SEMITES

Cultural Memory
in
the
Present

Mieke Bal and Hent de Vries, Editors

SEMITES

Race, Religion, Literature

Gil Anidjar

STANFORD UNIVERSITY PRESS

STANFORD, CALIFORNIA

2008

Stanford University Press
Stanford, California

© 2008 by the Board of Trustees of the Leland Stanford Junior University.
All rights reserved.

Printed in the United States of America on acid-free, archival-quality paper

Library of Congress Cataloging-in-Publication Data

Anidjar, Gil.
    Semites : race, religion, literature / Gil Anidjar.
        p.   cm.—(Cultural memory in the present)
    Includes bibliographical references and index.
    ISBN 978-0-8047-5694-5 (cloth : alk. paper)
    ISBN 978-0-8047-5695-2 (pbk. : alk. paper)
        1. Semites—History.   2. Semites—Religion.   3. Semitic
literature—History and criticism.   4. Antisemitism.   5. Christianity and
antisemitism.   6. Arabs—Public opinion.   7. Jewish-Arab relations.
8. East and West.   9. Orientalism.   I. Title.

GN547.A83 2007
306—dc22

                                                        2007001572

*To Amnon (Nono) Raz-Krakotzkin
with love and admiration*

Once again the Christian tradition, even in
secularized form, sought to distinguish itself from
Judaism and Islam by reassigning boundaries.
—Maurice Olender, *Languages of Paradise*

The current amazement that the things we are
experiencing are "still" possible in the twentieth
century is not philosophical. This amazement is
not the beginning of knowledge—unless it is the
knowledge that the view of history which gives
rise to it is untenable.
—Walter Benjamin, "Theses on the Philosophy of
    History"

Contents

Acknowledgments

By way of acknowledgment, a few notes on the circumstances of the writing of the essays that follow.

The first chapter was originally delivered at "tRACEs," a conference held at the University of California, Irvine, and organized by David Theo Goldberg and Dragan Kujundzic. I remain grateful for their invitation and for the opportunity to engage with the intense group of scholars they had gathered. The papers and discussions enabled me to learn much on the notion of race and to reflect on the Semites, the category I had left out of *The Jew, the Arab*, and one that could at once undo and buttress (all too hermetically, I feared) the argument I proposed there.

The restricted form of the chapter devoted to Edward Said, "Secularism" (chapter 2), is due to the fact that it was written as a homage to Said. As I write this, the essay is about to be published by *Critical Inquiry* thanks to the encouraging reading of W. J. T. Mitchell. I very much hope that the chapter, reproduced here by kind permission, retains the traces of its early intent. With it I mean to propose a reading of Said that highlights and reflects on his contribution to the "secularization" debate and to discussions on the rise of "religion" in democracy, in America and elsewhere, within the persistent context of Orientalism. The larger significance, whether or not I have succeeded in conveying it, resides in Said's life and work.

Chapter 3 has now been published in *Comparative Literature Studies* for a special issue on bilingualism edited by Rey Chow and Reda Bensmaïa, whom I very much thank for including me in the special issue of that journal. The chapter is reproduced here by kind permission. Inspired in part by Paul de Man's reflections on literature and modernity, the essay was presented at the Jewish Studies Seminar organized by Susannah Heschel at Dartmouth College. I am grateful for the invitation, for Heschel's generous hospitality, and for the opportunity to discuss the vexed question of relating Hebrew to Jewish literature from a variety of perspectives.

Chapter 4 was written at the kind request of Salma Khadra Jayyusi, whose stimulating idea to gather a series of studies on "classical narratives" in and around Arabic literature (the collection will be published soon under Jayyusi's editorial care) provided me with a welcome occasion to revisit and expand on literary questions that remain, to my mind, fruitfully open. Salma's support and generosity, as well as the range of her work, remain an inspiration.

I am grateful to Hent de Vries and to Norris Pope for the consistent support and rare expediency that has made the publication of this book possible. I am also indebted to Mitchell Hart for the subtle and helpful report he wrote for Stanford University Press, and to Emily-Jane Cohen, Tim Roberts, and Joe Abbott for impeccable handling and editing of the manuscript. I thank Larry Deyab for his amazing work and for his generosity in allowing me to use a photograph of his painting "Black Bridge (Falluja) 2005" on the cover (www.zieglergalerie.com/ld/ld_index.html). Marc Nichanian, Nina Caputo, Péter Szendy, Naveen Naqvi, Nauman Naqvi, and James Ingram have done more than they know (or that I have been able to tell them). Nermeen Shaikh makes everything possible and new. 'Eylam and Niv Anidjar, so far and so close, are an infinite source of joy and inspiration. Finally, Amnon (Nono) Raz-Krakotzkin, my very dear friend and teacher, has long provided me with sustained encouragement and uncommon support. A model of endless learning and enthusiasm, whether hearing, debating, or receiving earlier drafts—in whatever form or lack thereof—of the essays included in this book (and much more), Nono has taught me and given to me without counting and in a way that no expression of gratitude would suffice to acknowledge. But this insufficiency, I fear again, is more likely to be a measure of my limitations and failures. In order to mend some of these, I dedicate this book to him.

SEMITES

Introduction: Democracy in America

In democratic lands the moral power of the majority is immense, and the material strength at its disposal is out of property with that which is at first possible to gather against it. The party that sits in the seat of the majority, that speaks in its name and employs its power, therefore triumphs over all particular resistances in a moment and without trouble. It does not even allow them time to arise; it nips them in the bud.
—Tocqueville, *Of Democracy in America*

Before the "War on Drugs" and the "War on Terror" there was the "War on Witches." It was not, by any means, the first war of this sort, but it may serve as an example and an introduction to what Cotton Mather (one of the resident experts and leading intellectuals of those days) called "the Reality of Invisibles," particularly those with which the essays that follow are more directly preoccupied. Such wars have in fact identified and pursued their elusive and ephemeral objects, their inopportune targets, within a realm of doubtful perceptibility and persistent actuality. It is my hope, therefore, that there may be found in this brief rendering some usefulness toward introductory purposes.

Unwittingly marking a pregnant bicentennial—the year was 1692—Mather was intervening in the war on witches in order to assist "the endeavors of the Judges to discover and extirpate the authors of that Execrable witchcraft." It was urgent, he felt, to define the parameters of action and the rules of engagement. Later he would also warn against the door opened (doors—like walls—should always be closed) to excessive zeal and indiscriminate procedures that could themselves lead to the execution of individuals unjustly accused ("It is very certain that the devils have sometimes represented the shapes of persons not only innocent, but also very virtuous"). But first, a description of the war on these newly established domestic fronts: good, evil, and the bombing of buildings.

[S]o suppose a long train laid unto a barrel of Gunpowder under the floor where a neighbor is, & suppose a man with a match perhaps in his mouth, out of sight, set fire unto the further end of the train, though never so far off, this man also is to be treated as equally a malefactor [equally, that is "as that man is justly Executed for an Assassin, who in the sight of man shall with a sword in his hand stab his neighbor into the heart," as Mather had put it earlier]. Our neighbors . . . are blown up after a sort, with an infernal gunpowder, the train is laid in the laws of the Kingdom of Darkness. . . . Now the question is, Who gives fire to this train? & by what acts is the match applied? [F]ind out the persons that have done this thing, & be their acts in doing it, either mental, or oral, or manual, or what the Devil will, I say *abeant quo digni sunt* (Let them vanish where the righteous are).[1]

"Kill them all," Mather appears to rehearse in his unimpeachable Latin erudition harking back to the heyday of the Albigensian Crusade (and of more recent onslaughts as well); "God will recognize his own." The expandable targets here singled out as legitimate, offered as exemplary of *maléfice* and intended, if found guilty, "to be immediately exterminated," were like these murderous, if invisible, individuals who blow up buildings, those who light the long fuse (or "train") of infernal gunpowder. They are the evil bombers, whose mental, oral, or manual acts must be preemptively struck and ultimately destroyed, eradicated. They are (for "they" are many) witches, of course.

> This is how their world ends.
> This is how their world ends.
> This is how their world ends.

A few days after writing the letter from which I have been quoting, Mather joined a larger group of leading intellectuals and religious figures to make a public—a democratic—appeal. Together they voiced a poignant and impassioned argument for restraint ("there is need of a very critical and exquisite Caution") and for the protection of individual rights ("'tis necessary that all Proceedings thereabout be managed with an exceeding tenderness towards those that may be complained of"). This distinguished group was addressing itself to the executive branch and the higher powers to which it answered. They saw it as their priority to first express support and gratitude for the war on witches. Thereby demonstrating their love of the neighbor and of the neighborhood, these unelected representatives of a new election (of the voice of reason) pine for moderation as they congratulate the efforts of the local police and the coordinating activities of the different instances and agencies involved in this early version of Homeland Security: "We cannot but with all Thankfulness acknowledge, the Success which the merciful God has given unto the sedulous and assiduous Endeavors of our honorable Rulers, to detect the abominable Witchcrafts which have been committed in the Country; humbly praying that the discovery of these mysterious and mischievous Wickednesses, may be perfected."[2] The ministers then go on to insist on the important distinction between "matters of inquiry," "matters of presumption," and "matters of conviction," only the latter of which should serve for, well, conviction. Caution is thus required, especially if those under inquiry "have been Persons formerly of an unblemished reputation." As for the others . . . It is at any rate unclear to what extent the appeal was successful in this particular matter, or more generally. The burning of witches had already started, of course, but it did come to an end, in this case, albeit after much collateral damage.

The "Return of the Ministers" was not posted on www.petition-online.com ("more than 37 million signatures collected—thousands and thousands of active petitions," that Web site says). But witches are hardly the most obvious or pertinent example among those whom Talal Asad has described, after Stanley Diamond, as "conscripts of Western Civilization."[3] And though much is burning today, witches are no longer in the direct line of fire. In the following centuries other groups—internal or external enemies—would be targeted and identified as bringing danger to American shores. Others would be blamed for conspiring to light the fuse, accused of the fact that "our neighbors . . . are blown up after a sort, with an infernal gunpowder." The "city on a hill" remained true to the spirit—to the political theology—of the neighborhood and to the principle defined by Horkheimer and Adorno to the effect that "the mightiest" have always seen "in the victim the pursuer who has driven them to desperate self-defense" and the "weakest neighbor as an intolerable threat."[4] Still, what interest me are less the particulars of those identified and targeted as potential—literal or metaphorical—bombers, as evil ("the train is laid in the laws of the Kingdom of Darkness") and fanatical terrorists. I am preoccupied, rather, with the singular, if repeated, action and reaction of the victor and with the surrounding conditions, the operations of rhetoric, knowledge, and power deployed and applied. What are they doing, what are they *making*, those calling on witch burning (or the intensification of security measures, the retaliatory air bombing campaign and the blowing up of other neighbors, "Neighborhood Watch" style)? Those (but are they different? Cotton Mather certainly straddled both sides of that fence) calling for reform or restraint while recognizing, indeed, insisting that there *are* legitimate targets for "extermination" (a project, incidentally, that often involves very advanced, colored lenses or devices for identification purposes)? The question emerges because in the defensive and protective process that "endowed the afflicted with the power of life and death," in the "often explicitly Christological martyrdom of the afflicted," one scholar has claimed to find the constitutive origins of what she identifies as the American democratic personality. For Nancy Ruttenburg it is a matter of discovering—in an ineluctably Christian history, as well as in the empowerment of individuals to name the neighbor as witch (to partake in collectively legitimated denunciations, inform on her, in the name of love, as "America's Most Wanted," and finally burn her)—the making of the kind of democracy we have come to know and participate in, or "how democratization occurred historically on the microlevel of the individual subject."[5]

Recall, once again, the date and timing of the intervention. "The Return of the Ministers" is dated June 15, 1692, two centuries (and counting) after the onset of the largest genocidal enterprise in history (perpetrated, perhaps, in an earlier "fit of absence of mind") and five days after the first executions had started at Salem.[6] Operation "Inflicting Freedom" (or "Village Shield" or what have you) was already well on its way, and, the "Return" clearly asserts, it too was *justified*—by popular choice and by Christian faith. Hence, while hoping that, "in the Accusation of so many Persons," there may be "some [that] are yet clear from the great Transgression laid upon their charge," the ministers humbly ask for permission to insist and "recommend unto the Government, the speedy and vigorous Prosecution of such as have rendered themselves obnoxious, according to the Direction given in the Laws of God, and the wholesome Statutes of the English Nation, for the Detection of Witchcrafts."

The war on witches—the powerful assertion and the extended consequences of the doctrine of "the Reality of Invisibles"—was written as a chapter in the history of knowledge and in the history of power. It is a wide and efficacious, but by no means *universal*, history. Rather, and because "it is the access to universalization that grants a culture a hegemonic power,"[7] the war on witches is the history of American democracy (inside and outside its always expanding borders), as the self-appointed, and self-righteous, inheritor of tried-and-true European persecutory experiences; as maker and remaker of enemies as "social-imaginary institutions" that are "more *real* than the 'real.'"[8] There is no universal at work in the fact that, along with the evidence (spectral or other) that surrounded them, witches had to be detected and uncovered. They had to be made; they had to be studied (Cotton Mather even adopted a young girl, Martha Goodwin, for these human research purposes); they had to be feared and then burned: exterminated. In Gourgouris's words, "[F]oes are essentially legendary; even when real they are invariably constructed and reconstructed, *made legendary*."[9] And though the idea (or legend) of such foes has a long and all-too-respected lineage, the excesses of the uses to which it has been put—not to mention the historical delays and sheer empirical "details"—must be granted their singularity without subsuming the latter under some empty universal claim (of the sort: "anyone would have done the same thing had they only the power." But not everyone has, nor could one say with any assurance that anyone *would* have, say, exterminated Native Americans in their millions, enslaved Africans in their millions, gassed Jews in their millions, and so forth. Besides, what are the *benefits* of fabricating such universalizing claims about what might have been? And to whose advantage are they made?). There are no doubt innumerable gruesome chapters in the history of the world but none inherently universal, much less providing sufficient ground for historical, cultural, or ethical equivalence. Which is why we need to attend to the peculiarly Western, singularly Christian, history of knowledge and power that lingers on (would that it only lingered!) to this day. For multiple reasons, not least of which is the psychic, social, political, and theological investment daily manifested in our global, blown-up neighborhood, it seemed important to engage some of the responses to another "reality of invisibles," an uncannily dangerous group—now concealed, now visible, most often both at once—at the internal and external borders of the Christian West: the Semites.

That Semites constituted a danger—even if they were not simply exhausted by this particular attribute—is not to be doubted. Since Ernest Renan—another prominent intellectual honestly and candidly working the corridors of power—called for "the destruction of the Semitic thing [*la destruction de la chose sémitique par excellence*]," since he drafted anew and reiterated the declaration of "eternal war, the war that will not cease until the last son of Ishmael has died of misery or has been relegated to the ends of the desert by way of terror [*la guerre éternelle, la guerre qui ne cessera que quand le dernier fils d'Ismaël sera mort de misère ou aura été relégué par la terreur au fond du désert*]," Semites have remained an explosive locus—an opportune target for indiscriminate bombings—in the terror-filled Western imagination and, in less visible form (if not in less televised form), in its current geopolitical, or rather, theologeopolitical, order and incarnations.[10] To a large extent, or rather, to a quite complete extent, Semites were, like their ever so distant relatives—the Aryans—a concrete figment of the Western imagination, the peculiar imagination that concerns me in the chapters that follow. And just as the witches (the simultaneous efficacy and deep unreliability of "spectral evidence"), Semites were—I write in the past tense because Semites are a thing of the past, ephemeral beings long vanished as such—Semites were, then, something of a hypothesis (Chapter 1), contemporary with, and constitutive of, that other powerfully incarnate fiction named "secularism" (Chapter 2). Again, and as underscored by Edward Said, who raised anew the "Semitic question," the role of the imagination can hardly be downplayed.[11] It is the agent of invention in both its creative and destructive forms. Yet, as Talal Asad phrased it, "if invention always opens up the possibilities for difference, then it should also be clear that the conditions of invention are no longer what they once were."[12] This is why the second part in the small collection of essays presented here is further dedicated to the imagination, and more directly to the literary imagination, as a site of transformations, past and future (Chapters 3 and 4). It is there that one finds at their most manifest the conditions, the limits and openings, of something that could only perversely (not to say: wrongly) be called a "Semitic perspective."

Semites is, then, primarily a collection of essays, all of which aim to bring to a conclusion, however temporary and inadequate, the work I have joined in the past few years on the subject of Jews and Arabs. This is a subject that can be addressed from different perspectives, some of which I have tried to recall or explore, following the direction of others, in previous books.[13] Within my own limited trajectory *Semites* brings to its completion a trilogy of sorts, one unplanned and only retrospectively visible to me, by speaking to (and hopefully beyond) the earlier projects (roughly: *Our Place in al-Andalus*, dedicated to literary and rhetorical questions; and *The Jew, the Arab*, concerned with political and religious questions, matters of "race and religion"). This arbitrary moment of backward gazing hardly seems warranted, although it feels strangely unavoidable. It certainly does not mean to suggest anything like consistency between the parts of what now appears, at any rate, as an unintended three-part project. There have been changes of directions along with the persistence of earlier vectors (these should be readily recognizable). To the enduring and, to my mind, inescapable guidance I have found in the writings of Jacques Derrida and Edward W. Said has been added the increasing and formative influence of Talal Asad and Ashis Nandy, the growing sense of debt I feel toward them in my understanding of religion and politics, secularism, and the state. With them and others I share "the assumption that Western history has had an overriding importance—for good or ill—in the making of the modern world," the sense that "secularism is not simply an intellectual answer to a question about enduring social peace and toleration" but rather "an enactment by which a *political medium* . . . redefines and transcends particular and differentiating practices of the self that are articulated through class, gender, and religion."[14] With them and others I remain fascinated by the "internal colonialism" inherent to "the romance of the state" and by its persistence.[15] The way *Semites* seeks to inscribe itself in the margins of these thinkers and writers and of the issues they raise while pursuing earlier lines of inquiry (and, hopefully, concluding them) is by having two parts of equally important weight but asymmetric in terms of the three discursive spheres to which I obsessively return and that appear in the subtitle ("Race, Religion, Literature"). Part I, then, includes two essays on "race and religion" each of which engages a key moment in what Jacques Derrida has called "globalatinization" and Talal Asad has so compellingly described as "genealogies of religion" (the history of Christian knowledge and power). I try to contribute to the argument that in the nineteenth century were coagulated the conditions of emergence of the modern category of religion. I attend to the founding distinction that separated religion from race, a distinction that was at once built and collapsed on "the race who invented religion," namely, the Semites: Jews *and* Arabs. As the second chapter shows, Semites were equally, and surprisingly, instrumental in the rise and construction of secularism and of religion. Part II, finally, also contains two essays, but these, as I have already suggested, are most particularly dedicated to the literary imagination. Here I attend to the way in which the texts of Arabic and Jewish literatures undo the narrow limits to which they are confined by the topological imagination and by the disciplines—heirs to the "Semitic hypothesis" described in Chapter 1.

By insisting here on more or less "modern" developments, I do not mean to diminish, and much less dismiss, the earlier, iterative dimension of the divisions attended to throughout. When it comes to Jews and Arabs, and more generally to matters of race and religion, one would do well, in fact, to keep in mind the crucial force of repetition (with or without a difference), and particularly the resilience of older theologico-political patterns. To take but one major example, the significance of Hebraism—in the expansive sense of the term elaborated by Amnon Raz-Krakotzkin—can hardly be overstated as both prefiguring and sedimenting that which will later become modern Orientalism, the adoption of a Christian perspective on and by communities and practices, geographical and cultural areas.[16] More generally, the history of the "persecuting society," that of the "invention of world religions" and their relation to colonialism and to Western universalism (as Tomoko Masuzawa argues), consists in numerous historical chapters that are not without deep, and older, connections.[17] For those that preoccupy me here I claim no more than the strange privilege of an intensely visible invisibility. For who has not heard of the Semites? Who has failed to wonder about "anti-*Semitism*"? Who would deny the existence of Semites the way one confidently denies today that there are Aryan peoples? At the same time, who would dare bring Jews and Arabs under one, unproblematic, category? Who can ignore "Arab Jewish issues," collusions and separations—above all, separations—in whatever site or form, within whatever denegation or affirmation of increasingly doubtful expertise? Semites, then, and the conditions that have produced, divided, and effaced them, still have a hold on us.

PART I

SEMITES

The Semitic Hypothesis (Religion's Last Word)

> There is no racism without a language. The point is not that acts of racial violence are only words but rather that they have to have a word. . . . Racism always betrays the perversion of man, the "talking animal." It institutes, declares, writes, inscribes, prescribes. A system of marks, it outlines space in order to assign forced residence or to close off borders. It does not discern, it discriminates.
> —Jacques Derrida, "Racism's Last Word"

> The transference of a popular anti-Semitic animus from a Jewish to an Arab target was made smoothly, since the figure was essentially the same.
> —Edward Said, *Orientalism*

What Does a Christian Want?

The structural necessities made famous by Ferdinand de Saussure regarding the functioning and operations of a system of signs appear to have lost much of their currency. Yet there is reason to wonder whether the lesson was in fact learned. It remains, to announce the direction of the argument to follow, a deeply *historical* lesson that I will try to summarize in the best way I can. The difference introduced or constituted by a sign—any sign—within a system of signs (necessarily a differential system, since meaning is itself differential, a matter of relation between signs—and things, and even, if you will, "agents"), that difference must of necessity alter all relations, and therefore all the elements, within the system.[1] Whereas Saussure maintained that some differences mattered more than others (most memorably, the difference between *langue* and *parole*, as well as that between writing and orality), Derrida has demonstrated that any privileging of one sign or element (or of one difference—both of which will come under the term of *mark*, and there are others) above other marks is fundamentally, or rather structurally, *theological*. Not that there is anything wrong with theology. Only that, in this specific understanding, it isolates one sign (God, for example) and privileges the difference it makes, that is to say, one difference (e.g., divine vs. human), while asserting that this sign alone is not traversed or affected, itself not differentiated by other differential relations. Such privileging gestures, fixations of a dynamic, differential motion, which is nonetheless finite (which is itself another name for finitude), may be inevitable; structural necessities may even be inescapable. Resistance, in other words, may not only be futile; it may be impossible. Yet it is precisely in this impossibility that the possibility of change, for a change worthy of that name, as Derrida would say, resides. Because any sign and, further, any mark (constituted by the mark and the force of rupture of the mark) can break from its context (that is from the nonsystemic system, now understood as a finite, differential ensemble of marks), it can never be extracted from the differential motion that it is and of which it partakes. There resides in the mark the fact of repetition, citation and citationality, the fact (if it could be called such since it is itself a condition of possibility and impossibility of facts and events) of iterability that, more precisely, constitutes and deconstitutes the mark as what it is: the possibility and impossibility of the new, or, as Derrida put it, the possibility and impossibility of "revolutions that have as yet no model."[2]

In the finite grouping recently constituted by culture, race, gender, and class (or in Weberian fashion: science, morality, and art; but Fustel de Coulanges, Talal Asad explains, thought it was modern law, science, and politics), two terms have tended to remain invisible until quite recently, if in distinct ways. First is *religion*, which will occupy me throughout most of this chapter. Yet the other invisible term is, at this current juncture, more crucial to consider, for it determines the proclaimed novelty of the configuration.[3] That term, by now hegemonic, is *history*. Without being too formal about it we may remark that in this case history functions as either container or catalyst, as that within which or by way of which a new regime of marks and meanings comes about. History, in this extended and differential set of narratives, is often given the nickname of "modernity." To interrogate history, to interrogate the privilege it is granted in relation to other differences operative "in" it from a given moment (however extended, or even unfinished), is not to argue that there is no history nor change, no novelty or modernity. Rather, it is to ask about the way the historical, the modern, or better yet, historical *difference* "itself" is constituted as part of the differential regime within which one finds (or loses) oneself. It is the privileging of historical difference as the current theology of academic discourse that Derrida's work continues to call to our attention.[4] Again: it is not that there are no differences, be they historical, sexual, social, and even—if this may be conceded—racial, but rather that the way in which these (and other, always other) differences are constituted *as* historical, *as* sexual, and so forth must be interrogated in their very structure, operative mechanisms, and ways of deployment. The governing structure—that is to say, the mark or set of marks that silently governs and functions as if determining—implied by these specific modes of difference is what Foucault called *episteme*[5] and what Derrida, insisting on the failure and the finitude of any such governing mark or set of marks (including periodization), refused to call by one name (although he found it necessary at times to insist and underscore metaphysics, writing, dissemination, iterability, and even—but there are others, always others—religion) for the simple reason that any one is always already not one, more than one and no longer one, *plus d'un*.[6]

The difficulty thus engendered by analytic distinctions (themselves gendered) far exceeds binarism—which appears to have lost a significant part of its appeal anyway (if you exclude so-called patriots and their kind, the "us and them" kind) even if, to begin our approach toward religion, it has remained strangely fashionable to call for secularization and for renouncing "religion" (understood as a sort of pathological appeal to divine transcendence or authority)—a gesture that, given the modern distinctions of spheres and domains such as politics, science, ethics, aesthetics, economics, law, and, indeed, religion, would be comparable to proposing the altogether complete abandonment of collective investments in the ugly and the beautiful under the pretext that such terms are mistaken, or primitive, archaic and anachronistic, or still by themselves responsible for much too much violence in the world (which they are, of course).[7] Returning to the specific difference religion makes, then, within historical narratives the secularization thesis in the range of its possibilities may constitute an edifying illustration. Secularization has occurred, says Max Weber (and, more recently, Marcel Gauchet). The world is now disenchanted. Secularization has yet to occur, says Karl Löwith (and, more recently, if differently, Edward Said). We are still thinking according to religious or theological categories and methods. Secularization should not have occurred, says Carl Schmitt. Yet it has brought about a momentous change, a "translation" of devastating consequences from the theological to the political. Secularization is not the result of a translation, says Hans Blumenberg; religion only persists but metaphorically. And that's a good thing too.

None of the participants in this debate, summarily (and simplistically) represented here, deny that something new has occurred, that some momentous, indeed, decisive change has taken place. This change, they all tell us, took place historically (there lies historical difference), and it has to do with religion (a mark or ensemble of marks that, in this peculiar but widespread logic, has maintained enough integrity to still be called by the same name).[8] Another way to account for these arguments would be to describe historical change in more radical terms and to suggest that what used to be "religion" (if not quite called so) has become something else (rather than having disappeared into some metaphorical air). Thus Foucault, not so far from Schmitt's translation claim, argued locally that the role of the priest in the Catholic practice of confession was recast and recuperated by the psychoanalyst. More compellingly, perhaps, by way of a Foucauldian, analogical illustration (and not necessarily to suggest thereby that religion is a prison house), one could say that the prison, as a means of punishment, became an entirely different prison when it was turned into a means of education and discipline. Such a transformation, as Foucault shows, carries with it a generalized change in the very regime of marks articulated by and around notions such as sovereignty, power, law, health, education, self and subject, and, finally, man (and humanity). One need not be a nominalist to question the appellation *prison*, yet to assert continuities (or even, for that matter, ruptures) would come quite close to a fundamental misunderstanding regarding the advent of the new, of a novel regime of marks and meanings. Why, then, still call it a prison? Or, in our case, religion? (Either of these could hardly be reduced to "an enclosure within which human beings

are locked away," although I am certain that such is quite validly argu-
able, for both.) There are numerous reasons for the persistence of names,
but I would venture that among the *least* important are the so-called
choices made by scholars and intellectuals (including those who call for
abandoning both word and thing),[9] while among the most important
there is what William Hart, commenting on the work of Edward Said,
has called "the religious effects of culture," the by now very disciplined,
sedimented, and public need to renew and maintain identifications and
affiliations, to preserve existing structures by preventing confusion (the
political risk in confusing the prison with, say, the school should be as
obvious as the political gain of claiming that both are part of the benevo-
lent educational intent of the State).[10] At stake in this plural and collective endeavor are objective differences, and equally so, issues of economic
and political power, conditions of production, psychic investments (individual and collective), tensions and contradictions within the widest
cultural order, and so forth. To understand the educational system of
modern Western society, one must consider the lines of continuity (the
regimes of marks and meanings) tying together the school and the prison
as part of a disciplinary regime of "education."[11] Awareness of this link
may be lost as a result of privileging historical difference (under the guise
of the prison's "modernization") over differences between, say, disciplinary mechanisms and technologies of subjection and population management. Rather than the prison and the school, however, I want to explore
two no less disciplinary—albeit very different—marks, namely, religion
and race, and the strategic usages whereby one hides and obfuscates the
other. More precisely, I want to explore *the Semitic hypothesis.*

   I will, in a moment, engage some of the arguments relating religion
and race in the specific case of the Jews (arguments that, as Mitchell
Hart's work shows, must engage at once, if in novel ways, the two distinct scholarly projects entitled "the history of the Jews" and "the history of anti-Semitism").[12] It is not only that, as Gavin Langmuir has argued, the historical passage from religion to race described by Hannah
Arendt among others is insufficient to account for the history of anti-
Semitism;[13] it is also that the history of identifications (which includes
"self-identification," as well as surrounding perceptions) partakes of a
discursive regime, be this regime agonistic to the utmost in relation to

said identifications. To say this is akin to, but not identical with, Arendt's argument about discharging the victim of responsibility and should become clearer in what follows.[14] More to the point, for now, is the way in which race and religion have functioned internally and externally (and not only in the case of the Jews) as markers of historical shifts. Race and religion have functioned within what I have been referring to, after Derrida and Foucault, as governing regimes of marks and meaning.[15] The Semitic hypothesis, in this context, refers to the invention of the Semites, which is to say, the historically unique, discursive moment whereby whatever was said about Jews could equally be said about Arabs, and vice versa.[16] I refer to it as a "hypothesis," not only because I mean to recall scholarly deployments of the "Hamitic hypothesis" (the claim that one segment of the population of the African continent found its origin in a more civilized, northern race, which belonged to the reinterpreted biblical scheme of humanity, whereas autochthones would have belonged to a lesser, African, subhumanity) and its role in the colonization of Africa but because, as transient as any hypothesis, the Semites have had a strikingly ephemeral existence.[17] Except for the term *anti-Semitism*, debates over which have reached fairly ludicrous extremes (as in "who, really, were the Semites, and do Arabs have the right to claim they are Semites?" of the Bernard Lewis type),[18] the term and the idea have lost most of their currency. There are no more Semites today than there are Aryans, except in the discourse of marginal and isolated groups, if not entirely crazed individuals. The same development that has brought about this disappearance has also rendered obsolete the (public) claim that Jews are a race. Even the Jews' status as an ethnic group remains a difficult matter, at least in the United States, a fact to which testifies the enduring hegemony of the phrase "American Jews" over against the more ethnically inflected hyphenation "Jewish-American." Such a hyphenated claim would obviously include the Jews more squarely within the debates on ethnic identity and multiculturalism and would alter numerous (if not necessarily significant) political mappings.[19]

Regarding the other term of the Semitic hypothesis, namely, Arabs and Muslims, one could point to a distinct but parallel transformation, if also a difficult wavering, one rendered most visible, not so surprisingly, by Nazi policies. One could argue, in fact, that the Nazis at once produced the culmination and carried out the exhaustive demise of the notion of "Semites." Having learned all they could from their predecessors and Orientalist teachers regarding Aryans and Semites, the Nazis not only brought about the actualization of that lesson; they fundamentally altered it, changing its shape for the following generations. Whereas in keeping with the racial discourse that had been elaborated by the nineteenth century, the Nazis thoroughly racialized and detheologized the Jew ("For actually the Mosaic religion is nothing other than a doctrine for the preservation of the Jewish race," wrote Hitler in *Mein Kampf*), and they can also be credited with having completely deracialized Islam.[20] One has to reflect, therefore, on the patent lack of interest manifested by Hitler and other Nazi ideologues at the time regarding those hard to ignore Semites, which the Arabs were unanimously considered to be (I am obviously not suggesting that Arabs did not register on their persecutory scales). Prior to any anti-British interests, the Nazis had learned their "philological" lessons well. They did classify Arabs as Semites, but they also had personal and political interests in Islam,[21] which they appear to have considered strictly and narrowly as a religion (and a praiseworthy, martial religion at that), emphatically *not* as a racial marker.[22] What had been for Ernest Renan virtually the selfsame Semites (Jews and Arabs), at once race and religion, became for the Nazis highly differentiated groupings, differentiated in the very terms and deployments of race and religion—a distinction that had all but disappeared precisely under the very term *Semites*. Unsettling as it may be, the Nazis thereby started a "trend" that remains operative today. Islam, the religious dimension of which the West had so stubbornly resisted acknowledging (recall Othello), became fully established as the paradigm of religiosity (as were the Semites). The Jews, on the other hand, never quite recovered their privileged religious identity and were displaced and replaced ("recognized," as was, by then, said) in their "eternal" political longings (so strangely similar to the latest European versions of ferocious ethnic nationalism, as Hannah Arendt argued early on),[23] or to America, where they also became "white folks," albeit in a different manner from Ashkenazi Israelis.[24] In this context the historical configuration whereby within two years after the publication of *Mein Kampf* the Hebrew University of Jerusalem established the first two of its institutes may appear in a sharper light. Indeed, by distinguishing epistemologically and institutionally the study of Judaism from the study of the Arab and Islamic Orient, the Hebrew University—representative of a general Zionist outlook—initiated an academic trend that would be sealed in the post–World War II academic world of the United States.[25] More important, for now, as religion and race became more and more distant, more effective in their mutual concealment and disciplinary effects, so did Jews and Arabs become increasingly distinct, less and less Semitic, thus returning to a very different, if more familiar, state of affairs in which everything separates the two as less than kin *and* less than kind enemies (recall Shylock *and* Othello).[26]

Another essential element in the appearance and disappearance of the ephemeral Semites is the fact that they existed in European consciousness for precisely as long as Europe thought of itself as resolutely secular, as having achieved secularization (following, as some scholars have suggested, "the last religious century," the eighteenth century). "Le caractère du XIXe siècle," writes Renan, "c'est la critique."[27] As religion is said to wane in the West, it is the East that emerges and becomes "religion" (under the figure of "the Mystic East"), or, as Marx had already remarked, the history of the East appears as a history of religions.[28] This is the history of the theologico-political as the history of the enemy (distributed along topographic and geopolitical lines—the Jew, the Arab), a history that has resumed with a vengeance, when the State of Israel (but there are others) continues to be thought of as secular, politically modern, and democratic (except for crazed "fundamentalists," who remain a limited, if dangerous, minority); and its "enemies" are considered as religious fanatics lacking political claims, democratic culture, and whatnot. They are not a race, barely a civilization (*pace* Samuel Huntington), but they constitute, quite clearly and certainly, a religion (albeit an aberrant and irrational one). Once equally Semites, Jews and Arabs were both race and religion in a secular political world—fantasmatic and imaginary as the latter was and remains. Today, and since Nazism at least, one can divide them again, divide the world between political entities, religious ones, and racial (or cultural) ones. And who would dare deny that religious distinctions, indeed, religious identifications, hide the most persistent remnants of a history of racism? Clearly, racism has not disappeared, and neither has religion, but this puzzling fact remains: the Semites are no longer. And it will be impossible to understand this disappearance without considering Edward Said's insight that "perhaps, religion, like Orientalism, is a discourse, a distinctively Western way of thinking, of formulating and organizing concepts, of relating particular words and particular things."[29] Think, for example, of his reminder that this—race, religion: the Semites—is the history of Europe (*not* of the East or of the Middle East, even if it has had and continues to have devastating consequences on these "areas"), the history of what the Christian wants (think of the debate around *l'affaire du foulard* in France and of the opposition to Turkey's entry into the EEC, merging with a renewed affirmation of Europe's Christian identity; but think of "the war on terror"; think, if you must, of Bush as well, and think of Sharon and his successors, of Israel's alliance with Christian evangelists and their joined bombing campaigns; think of the claim that there is no opposition to "Islam" in the war against "fanatic terrorists," and think of U.S. military presence in the Middle East among other places, and think, if you will, that there is no racism in that; think of the fact that "Arabs" are not considered a distinct ethnic group in the administrative forms of the American immigration services, but that is already changing—and not for the better; think about others). *Wo es war*, as Freud might have said, or: Where religion has emerged, race has all but disappeared (that is to say that though visible, it has been concealed in its power and effects); where politics are seen as determining, religion has all but disappeared (that is to say that though visible, it has been concealed in its power and effects). It was not always so. And so, again, the Jew, the Arab—and there are others. This, then, is the Semitic hypothesis in its crudest form: secularism is Orientalism. Race is religion. The evidence lies in the Semites.

Jews

There is little reason to interrogate the assertion that modern racism and modern anti-Semitism are one and the same phenomenon. However one defines *race*, it is undeniable that, in modern times, Jews came to be considered a race.[30] It is only thanks to the groundbreaking work of Mitchell Hart, however, that one is now able to measure the extent to which European Jews themselves, and, for the most part, Zionists, kindly prodded by a great number of eager Jewish scholars, enthusiastically embraced the definition of their Jewishness as race.[31] Along with the emergence of the notion of "Jewishness," then, Jews (and paradigmatically for Sander Gilman, Freud) came to be identified as well as to identify themselves as members of a race, linked, as Freud put it, by a "strong feeling of solidarity with my people (*mit meinem Volk*)."[32] Although Gilman and others have also traced the nonlinear history that additionally conceived of Jews as a differently gendered group (something of a "third sex"),[33] racial (which means sexual as well) categorizations seem to have dominated Jewish group identity in the twentieth century all the way to the Nazi camps, and further with Zionism and the State of Israel. This did not go without a struggle as other Jewish groups had been advocating a different, no less novel, understanding of their Jewishness, offering instead an equally recent "Judaism," this time as a religion.[34]

I have already suggested that there is a larger methodological point to be made on the basis of Mitchell Hart's work on this particular historical chapter. To trace a history of the identifications of Jews, which goes beyond an inventory of "cultures of the Jews," would be a mammoth enterprise that would have to engage not only what Jews have written, made, or practiced of themselves but weighty moments—discursive regimes—within which so-called self-perceptions are articulated. Hence, and to remain within a very limited geographical area, it becomes necessary to address the Jews' theological status as "witnesses" in Western Christendom; the subsequent and later representation of Jews as demonic figures excluded from theological jurisdiction; their becoming protected property of the Crown in medieval Europe, a class of sorts; the dissemination of conceptions of blood as a determining mark of nobility or infamy, and the "disciplinary revolution" constituted by the Spanish and Portuguese Inquisitions;[35] Spinoza's refiguration of the Hebrew Bible as "a national standard of right,"[36] a "rule of right living" (39), the "special constitution of [the Jews'] society and government" (47) (into which Moses "introduced a religion, so that the people might do their duty from devotion rather than fear" [75]), that is to say, an obsolete political constitution of which Jews would be the obsolete followers; Kant's puzzlement as to what it would mean to recognize in "the Palestinians living among us (*die unter uns lebender Palästiner*)" a nation of merchants that may or may not be further united by a constitution, rites, and language,[37] and further Marx's view that the Jews are the generalization of a particular class interest that has been adopted by, and has come to dominate, the Western, Christian world;[38] and finally (for the purposes of this chapter) Hegel (closely followed by more or less vocal admirers like Ernest Renan and William Robertson Smith), who saw in Jews a paradigm of religiosity, indeed, an essential link in a religious (if not sacred) history that led to Christianity and beyond. All such views (the "anti-Semitism" or "anti-Judaism" of which should not be too easily, or unreflectively, granted) would have to be taken into account in order to narrate a history of the Jews. This is so not only because these moments are essential to an understanding of the place of the Jews in Western Europe but also because those who called themselves and were called "Jews" were either the source of, or came at one moment or other to, these identifications. Throughout these changes, one might point to continuities (Spinoza, for example, granted two constant elements, circumcision and hatred), but any affirmation concerning the substance of these continuities would also have to determine what its substrate was (and whether it was itself unchanging) on which changes occur.[39] The easiest, most banally obvious, answer, before "Judaism" or other so-called abstractions, would have to be, or so it seems, "the Jews."

This is not as far-fetched as it sounds and does find a strange confirmation in a somehow unexpected place. At the time they were being murdered by the Nazis, argues Hannah Arendt, "there was not the slightest doubt that Jews had been killed *qua* Jews."[40] In a gruesome parody of "l'art pour l'art," a particularly perverse moment of the " aestheticization of politics," Jews would have been attacked and killed, reduced to the very substrate of their otherwise historically changing and highly textured existence: qua Jews. To be sure, Arendt by no means endorsed the view that anti-Semitism was an unchanging phenomenon or any such kind of Jewish essentialism. In fact, the importance of her argument resides precisely (if not only) in her opposing such perceptions. Nonetheless, Arendt here appears to join a quite impressive choir in the modern rhetoric of victimology (as a specific contribution of modern racism), namely, that those targeted were or are persecuted and attacked *for who they are.*

Was this, however, the case? Would it not be necessary, for example, to admit that the Nazis did not define their targets merely as unbearable existential facts, simply as Jews? The Nazis did *arrest* people as Jews, that is, people they called Jews (*as if* they were, which sometimes they weren't); but however despicable and horrifying their definition of "the Jew" was, the Nazis did have a more elaborate one than that fact of existence as such. Nazis "knew" (that is, they claimed or thought they knew) what Jews were, and what they were for them had little to do with (even if it was not entirely independent from) the ways in which Jews conceived of themselves. That is why the Nazis could identify as "Jews" scores of people who had absolutely no relation to Jews, people who made no claim to Jewishness, not because they were hiding, afraid, ashamed, or self-hating but because it would never have occurred to them to identify with any Jewishness whatsoever. Here lies the clearest and, to my mind, most devastatingly misinterpreted evidence as to the crucial discrepancy between "Jew" as uttered and defined by the Nazis and "Jew" as uttered by, well, everybody else (even taking account of obvious contaminations, recontextualizations, lack of hermetic distinctions, and so forth). This evidence is to be found in the early and by now highly disparaged reaction of German Jews (today, and for quite some time already, paradigmatically described as no more insightful than bumbling idiots regarding their inevitable fate), who simply could not believe that the Nazis could ever have meant *them* when they uttered the word—that is to say, the death-sentence—*Jew*. To speak of the persecutions of the Jews under the Nazis as the persecution of Jews qua Jews is to suggest that the given identity of the victim is truthfully confirmed (rather than fantasmatically, if effectively, enforced) by the persecutor.

I call Arendt's argument unexpected, indeed, surprising because it collapses two distinct discursive moments in the extension of the Nazi death sentence. The first is the recognition by the persecuted addressees that there is no escape from that sentence, that having been targeted (identified) leaves them with no options (modern racism is often recognized by its targeting of an inescapable given). The second moment, that that to which one is reduced at that moment is *what one is*. Elsewhere, it is precisely this second moment of recognition ("I am that name") that Arendt will poignantly isolate as far from granted and rather uphold in its political significance and specificity. "In times of defamation and persecution," she writes in her Lessing Prize lecture, there is "a political fact" that must be established in and at the very moment of persecution. "Nowadays," to claim such a fact through one's actions "would seem like a pose." And perhaps it is. Yet in what Arendt calls "dark times," this "pose," as the assertive making of a political fact, is precisely what must be assumed in the name of a basic and simple principle: "the principle that one can resist only in terms of the identity that is under attack." One may reject such collective identifications, says Arendt (as if to emphasize that the discourse of the persecutor is not what is decisive, that there remains a choice, indeed, a rupture between the insult, the threat, and the attack, on the one hand, and its reception, on the other), but it would mean abandoning the political world and escaping into an imaginary one or worse. These escapees would, in that way, "feel wonderfully superior to the world, but their superiority is then truly no longer of this world; it is the superiority of a more or less well-equipped cloud-cuckoo-land."[41] Politics, for Arendt, would thus mean confronting and engaging one's persecutor on the very terrain, on the battleground and war theater, he has chosen; it is to respond to the persecutor in the world—in *his* world, such as he has made and unmade it—with no possibility of escape, with no other world toward which to turn. It is in this world, the only world there is, Arendt tells us, that religion becomes race, that the distinction between them is not only sedimented but inscribed as temporally distinct and distant.

Religion and Race

Beyond the dispute regarding the history of the term, its numerous meanings and usages across the centuries, there is no question that, as Jonathan Z. Smith argues, a momentous change—or shall one better say, a momentous beginning—is initiated in the sixteenth century. "The term 'religion' has had a long history," writes Smith, "much of it, prior to the sixteenth century, irrelevant to contemporary usage."[42] It is also the case that religion (its referent or referents—were there one or many?—and adjectives) became a question "in response to an explosion of data," an explosion that grew exponentially in the nineteenth century with the establishment, throughout Western Europe and North America, of chairs of philology and, indeed, religion. In fact, it is altogether "a different set of taxonomic questions [that] were raised by the 'religions' and [which] became urgent by the nineteenth century" (275). Why urgent? And why that change precisely then? Smith does not engage, in this essay, the question of "secularization" or, more precisely (in Frank Manuel's formulation), the paradoxical fact that "one might call the epoch of Voltaire and Hume the last religious century."[43] In Smith's analyses it is as if the interest in "religion" emerges outside of a history of what happens to Christianity in the West, outside of what may be called, no less paradoxically, the first (and perhaps the only) secular century.[44] Elsewhere, in the same collection of essays, another distinguished scholar of religion, Gustavo Benavides, engages this very historical issue under the heading of "modernity." There, if only by way of consequences, Benavides signals toward a fundamental fact in the study of religion, tying it to that same century and to the contemporary and rapidly coagulating discourse of race and ethnicity: "A study of the so-called world religions, *a term used to refer to those religions that do not serve primarily as vehicles for ethnic identification*, shows that many of the concerns that characterize Western modernity appeared as the result of the caesura established by the religious founders' skepticism toward received ideas and practices."[45]

The view that religion and ethnicity, indeed, religion and race, are either indifferent and even opposed to each other has a long history that may go back to the perception that "early Christians neither defined themselves nor were perceived in terms of race or ethnicity," in the claim that "the foundations, the very definition of earliest forms of Christianness, *depend upon the rejection* of race or ethnicity."[46] A schematic, and popular, confirmation of this view can be found in assertions concerning persistently diverging notions of kinship and of community. Whatever the historical value of such assertions, they already establish that between Christianity and Judaism (hardly in existence at the time as separate entities, as Daniel Boyarin has demonstrated) the difference is not symmetrical, that they do not locate themselves on the same plane of existence. One, for example, would consider itself in religious, spiritual terms, the other in ethnic, bodily terms. To add to the equation by way of different conceptions of gender and sexuality, distinct modes of social divisions and of political order, political power, maintain, if only analytically, distinct spheres of existence.[47] Here, too, the question of a substrate on which distinctions are elaborated comes into play. By the time the question of "religion" and "religions" will take shape in the early modern period, that is to say, by the time "religion" will be invented as a distinct category of understanding, so will race and ethnicity. Is it necessary to recall that religion is therefore an essential moment of colonial knowledge, an essential tool of colonial power?[48] To the extent that one can speak of "the invention of the prison," the same word (which should not suggest a creation out of nothing) can profitably be invoked to speak of the contemporary invention of religion and race. A crucial moment of this invention—a contentious one, to be sure—registers in the exponential increase of interest in "the Orient" and its "religions," once again, in the nineteenth century: "The plural 'religions' has been even more contentious. In the nineteenth century this idea was refined and its scope expanded. The three 'revealed religions'—Christianity, Judaism, Islam—remain as the Western religions, while the imprecise 'heathenism' became the so-called Eastern and primal religions. 'Eastern religions' were born in the Western imagination in the early 1800s—'Boudhism' in 1821, 'Hindooism' in 1829, 'Taouism' in 1839, and 'Confucianism' in 1862."[49]

The "invention of these religions," as Peter Harrison calls it—and its distinction from, its apparent lack of connection with, the invention of modern racism—must, however, be understood as an inclusive, disciplinary mechanism, a strategy of sorts that distributes and separates according to distinct and apparently unrelated grids of differences, religious differences and ethnic or racial differences. I am talking here of discipline, that is to say also but not only academic disciplines (religious studies and ethnic or cultural studies).[50] The example of the Jews, discussed above, is thus meant to interrogate the historicization of such differences, which functions within scholarly discourse but also outside of it in popular (and not so popular) discourse, and operates in a circular manner so as to establish, sediment, or simply confirm the difference between religion and race, as if one was historically older or more natural than the other.[51] In this case, to consider that the Jews *became*, if contentiously, a race is not inaccurate, but it does inscribe religion as the "older" category rather than recognize that religion and race are *contemporary*, indeed, coextensive and, moreover, co-concealing categories.[52]

Semites

Hesitations and waverings around the names and designations that would "properly" describe the past and current situation in Israel/Palestine are, I have argued elsewhere, well known, and they say much about the agenda served by each alternative, consciously or not. Who, after all, are the adversaries? Israelis and Palestinians? Jews and Muslims? Jews and Arabs? Political realists and religious extremists? By now notably less invisible than the term *Aryan*, which appears to have survived under different guises in linguistics and philology (from which it emerged in the first place) and marginal groupings, the term *Semites* has nonetheless lost much of its currency even if popular perceptions continue to construe the issue in its highly segregated neighborhood, in the vicinity of European racial and racist phantasms. Today, the terms *Jew* and *Arab*—echoes of not so distant shadows—remain dominant, lingering effects of an "archive of paradise," as Maurice Olender puts it. Yet it is not just that the shift marked by these terms produces a partial "excision" of race.[53] Rather, the discursive shift from *Semites* to *Jew* and *Arab* rewrites fantasmatic alliances and refigures the distinction between race and religion, religion and politics, and ethnicity and race, while occluding or even excising, as it were, the Aryan and the racist elements from the equation. More important, perhaps, the shift both produces and sediments ancient oppositions along even older theologico-political tracings, rendering its history invisible.

At a most practical level, the terms *Jew* and *Arab* remain dominant not only because they constitute the lexicon according to which both the "conflict" and its alleged solutions are articulated (hence, the popularity of the two-states solution, one Jewish, one Arab or Palestinian, as if these terms were simply opposites, even clearly distinguishable) but also because they have long determined the daily life of millions by having been inscribed on Israeli ID cards since the earliest years of the State of

Israel.[54] There, Jew or Arab come before the law and under the heading "nationality"—this latter category thereby distinguished from "citizenship," that is, "Israeli." In Israel, then, *Jew* would continue to function as a religious, albeit detheologized, term, whereas *Arab* would appear to be distinct from any religious content, an ethnic and political marker, a racial and even racist category that functions as a screen for, among other things, "Muslim fanaticism" or simply (although this is anything but simple) "religion."

In a proximate context Bernard Lewis documents the Eastern European genealogy of the modern distinction between nationality (i.e., ethnic nationality) and citizenship, a distinction that sediments ethnicity, culture, and ultimately race into the prepolitical ground of citizenship. Lewis also points out that the institutionalization of this distinction involved the transformation of religion into ethnicity (in our case, *Jew*), and a confinement, even a kind of eradication of religion (here, *Arab*, which stands for, and erases, Muslim or Christian) as an identity category. The significance of this "secular" institution that would leave religion behind in the historical distance finds its origin, as we saw, in the nineteenth century's "denial . . . of the solely religious character of Jewry, and the attempt to redefine Jewry along national/racial lines."[55] It belongs to the long history that, meticulously documented by Olender in *Languages of Paradise*, invented the "Semites." The distinction between nationality and ethnicity, which also "erases" religion, can be traced, as a specific political practice, to the Soviet Union (and, earlier still, to colonial regimes). The pragmatic, if not historical, reasons for this political inscription are made clear in Lewis's comment that "ethnic nationality, unlike religion, cannot be changed by an act of conversion."[56] Whether one speaks, therefore, of Israelis and Palestinians (nationalism as the primary factor), Jews and Muslims (religion as the primary factor), or Jews and Arabs (ethnically defined, with poised, "democratic" *politics* on one side and "fanatical" *religion* on the other), one is never simply mistaken but maintains rather a state of affairs that, institutionalized by the State of Israel as a culmination of a difficult and still unwritten history, reinscribes invisible or uninterrogated distinctions between and within race and religion, religion and politics, and finally, between and within Semites, the Jew, the Arab.

Edward Said has famously attended to Orientalism as part of "a secular post-Enlightenment myth whose outlines are unmistakably Christian," the European invention of, among others, these Semites, a unique and somewhat changing, if ephemeral, figure whereby the Jew and the Arab merge into one ("Arabs are simply Jews on horseback, and all are Orientals at heart" comments Said on Disraeli's *Tancred*).[57] "The Christian tradition," writes Maurice Olender in turn, "even secularized, wished one more time to define itself vis-à-vis Judaism and Islam by reassigning roles, by drawing the borders."[58] Figuring, at first, a linguistic division, Semites and Aryans quickly became racial markers, markers that also persisted in articulating a theologico-political difference, which Europe could locate as historically and geographically distant (the Middle Ages or the Middle East). Announcing the transformation of the Jews into a religious community as well as into a political one, as if unaware of the distinction, J. G. Herder granted the *ancient* Hebrews both religious and political expression. To the (modern) Jews, this "Asiatic people," he granted only a political future, one that may take place on the land of Palestine.

After Herder, Ernest Renan ("probably the first to oppose the 'Semites' to the 'Aryans' in a decisive '*division du genre humain*'")[59] emphatically considered Hebrews, Jews, Arabs, and other Semites as a race locked out of any political organization, one frozen in the past of a religious desert, a race that produced nothing but the strictest and driest of monotheisms. "It is impossible to understand Israel well," Renan writes, "without tying it back to the group of peoples of which it is a part, by which I mean, the Semitic race."[60] Renan thus introduced "racial categories into theological discussions," providing "an important religious legitimation for the rise of racial anti-Semitism in the 1880s."[61] To the extent that he was instrumental in establishing the grounds of "Semitic philology," as well as in producing extensive descriptions of the Semitic race (as opposed to the Aryan race), Renan also blurred the lines and collapsed newly elaborated racial and religious differences that had recently become common in scholarly and popular discourse. To that extent Renan's claim as to a total absence of a political dimension in the Semites bears a structural, if inversed, similarity to Herder's gesture that upheld the political over the religious on the basis of a previous undistinguishability. Renan's bears an even more rigorous affinity to William Robertson Smith's collapse of religion and politics.

Consider, for example, how what begins as a parallel and an analogy between two spheres rapidly becomes one undistinguishable whole. Robertson Smith writes: "The parallelism in ancient [Semitic] society between religious and political institutions is complete."[62] At this point there would therefore seem to be two "spheres" ("In each sphere," Smith continues, "great importance was attached to form and precedent"). The correction of that impression follows immediately: "Strictly speaking, indeed, I understate the case when I say that the oldest religious and political institutions present a close analogy. It would be more correct to say that they were parts of one whole of social custom" (21). The difference between religion and politics thus becomes irrelevant, something that will not prevent Smith from insisting that his is an exclusive inquiry into the "religion" of the Semites.[63]

It is the same Semites, the same peculiarly religious race (which he would be "the first to acknowledge . . . truly represents an inferior configuration of human nature"),[64] that Renan credits with bringing about the discovery, "without reflection nor reasoning," of the purest religious form humanity had ever known.[65] This discovery was, to be sure, anything but an invention: "[o]n n'invente pas le monothéisme." Rather, a kind of "primitive intuition" enabled the Semites to part from the world in a unique way and arrive, "without any effort" or mediation, at the notion of the Supreme God. "This great conquest was not for them the effect of progress or of philosophical reflection: it was one of their first apperceptions" (87). Defined by (and, one would almost want to say, *as*) religion, the Semitic nomad is thus both "the most and the least religious of human beings."[66] Undeniably a race (although Renan himself was adamant that he used the term in a more sophisticated than merely biological sense),[67] "a race so highly gifted to create religions and disseminate them," the Semites have "neither plastic arts, nor rational science, neither philosophy nor political life, nor even military organization." In short, "la race sémitique n'a jamais compris la civilisation dans le sens que nous attachons à ce mot."[68] There is an abyss (not a clash of civilizations, since Semites do not constitute one), a chasm between Aryan and Semite, the chasm that separates religious origins from political growth, the dried-out and distant source from its fruitful, proximate outcome. The width of this abyss is matched, however, only by the proximity, the quasi-identity, of Jew and Arab. What Renan calls "the Semitic spirit" has in fact only two "pure forms," namely, "the Hebraic or Mosaic form, and the Arabic or Islamic form."[69] As he further explains, indifferently gathering Semitic illustrations from Hebrew and Arabic and from Jewish and Arabic traditions, "the Jew [is] like the Arab" and vice versa.[70] Ancient Israel thus gives us "la vie arabe dans toute sa perfection" (91). Equally vengeful, both Solomon and Muhammad are paradigmatic of the "Semitic type" (94), and both are political failures, incapable of maintaining a state. "The history of Israel is no longer that of a state, but of a religion. Such is the fate of people who must fulfill an intellectual or religious mission toward other peoples, that they must sacrifice their nationality to this brilliant and dangerous vocation" (108). The missionary people have "no other country [pas d'autre patrie] than this thought" (109). They can have, therefore, no political claims (clearly, for Renan, Zionists could not be Semites, and Palestinians could not ask for a State—not so much has changed after all).

If the Semites invented religion, the Aryans invented politics, science, the arts, and really everything else. Continuing a practice launched most vocally perhaps by Hegel ("Arabs and Jews," Hegel wrote, "have only to be noticed in an external and historic way")[71] and publicly defended by Renan, nineteenth-century Orientalists all but equate Jew and Arab and credit them, as I have said, with nothing but the most abstract discovery of, the most innate instinct for, *religion*. A race devoid of political history, their cultural sterility akin to a monotheistic desert, the Semites constitute the clearest site of a distinction produced by the only century that genuinely believed itself "secularized." When the distinction between religion and politics becomes irrelevant (either because they are so thoroughly distanced from each other as to become irrelevant or because they have so entirely collapsed as to become indistinguishable), the Jew and the Arab merge, one religious race at last (valued positively, as in Disraeli, or negatively, as in Renan). Rereading a history of the Semites from Hegel's "religions of the sublime" to Rosenzweig's "messianic politics" by way of political Zionism, one witnesses this Orientalist imaginative feast, this invention articulated around the disappearance of a distinction (between Jew and Arab, race and religion), followed by the renewed separation of Arab from Jew and, finally, by the transformation of the Arab into the Jew's "creeping, mysteriously fearsome shadow" so soberly attended to by Edward Said.[72] Theologico-political fault lines, as well as racial ones, clearly remain determining in spite (and perhaps because) of the "Semitic" hiatus, as they remain determining of what has been called "Jewish Orientalism" and, indeed, of Zionism and the Zionist state. Siding with the West, Zionism and its affiliated scholars sought (still seek) to reintegrate "history" and to liberate themselves from the distant East, to integrate the European community by reproducing it, to liberate themselves, first, from Judaism itself (that nineteenth-century invention that, aside from scientific subtleties, took pride—among other contributions to world civilization—in its Islamic offshoot),[73] from a Judaism that potentially signified a "bi-national" Arab Jewish existence; second, from Islam; and, finally, internally and externally, from the Arabs. At stake, then, would be the anti-Semitism of Zionism, which, seeking the End of Exile, *shlilat ha-galut*, strives to bring to its conclusion the alleged ahistoric (non)existence of the "exilic" Jew, be he the Oriental, *Mizrahi*, Jew, or the no less Oriental Eastern Jew, *Ostjude*, both equally diasporic Jews and no more than obstacles to the "new Jew."[74] No less Orientalistic than its elders in its conceptions of the East, no less anti-Semitic than the rest of the Christian West, Zionism more pointedly reinscribes what was already at work in the early invention of the Semites: the European wedge that, now called "secularization," would turn away from religion, distance itself from the only invention of its Semitic, monotheistic, and desertic origins ("Les Juifs dehors!"—Herzl heard in Paris and, upholding the imperative, called on Jews everywhere to abide), and separate race from religion, and religion from (modern) politics, separate, finally, the Jew from the Arab. Political Zionism, then, is another name for the beginning and end of the "Semite," its paradoxically double internalization and exteriorization. The enemy within, the enemy without: the Arab, out of the Jew, and the Jew, out of Europe, exported, deported.

Jews and Arabs

What needs to be interrogated, again and again, is the becoming-
enemy, the history of the (religious, political, ethnic, and racial) enemy
that is inscribed within and between the polarized identities of Jew and
Arab. If it constitutes a history, it is one that is longer than a colonial
one, although colonial dimensions—the implication, indeed, the founding and continuing role of British colonialism and American imperialism, to mention only two prominent actors, in the creation and the
continuation of the "Middle East conflict"—are perhaps better known
and better studied, if not necessarily better understood. But more puzzling, perhaps, than the chapters of this history is the question of why
that history has not been written. Beyond a horridly all-too-familiar and
inescapable "cycle of violence," what is it that maintains the distance and
kindles the enmity between the Arab and the Jew? What purposes are
served by, what are the reasons for, the naturalization of this distance,
the naturalization of the opposition, of the enmity between Arab and
Jew, one that, as prominent narratives would have us believe, goes back
to ancient biblical times, the ineluctable legacy of "the Middle East," a
region and a land eternally ravaged by war and conflict? How did the
ostensible markers of Arab (an "ethnic" marker) and Jew (a "religious"
one) come to inscribe themselves so forcefully on modern discourses of
the most varied kind—political, religious, cultural, and so forth—even
when accompanying distinct or even opposed political agendas, caveats,
and sophisticated critiques and debunkings?

Most analyses of the "Middle East conflict" have focused on Europe's oft-noted export of the "Jewish question," thereby considering the
choice of Arab Palestine as a contingency of European colonialism or as
a result of Zionist aspirations. Other, important analyses attend to the
transformations of another history, the history of the opposition between
"Islam and the West." To put it schematically, the first analyses attend
to anti-Semitism, on the one hand, the latter to Orientalism (although
Edward Said rightly insisted that he was attending to both).[75] Without
diminishing the accuracy of these accounts, nor the injustice involved in
making Palestinians pay for the guilt of Europe vis-à-vis the Jews, one
must nonetheless consider that these accounts entirely take for granted

distinct states of enmity (between Jews and Arabs, between Europe and the Arabs, between Europe and the Jews, compounded in this last case by some eternally irreparable guilt) while ignoring the possibility of hidden links and explicit associations (not simply potential comparisons, however outrageous or justified) between these pairings.[76] They forgo explanation of the very historical problem that enmity poses, failing to engage the three "elements" at once (Europe, the Jew, the Arab), failing to engage both religion and race. They presuppose, for example, and without interrogating it, the separation of two groupings, "Europe and the Jews" and "Islam and the West" (to quote two celebrated subject headings), and reinscribe the stability of an "idea" of Europe (one that remains as fragile today as it ever was, even at its most violent moments of enforced identity), an idea that would exist without necessary relation to the Jew and/or the Arab. Finally, these accounts also take for granted the distinction of Arab and Jew as two polarized identities having been constituted independently of each other. There is no point in denying that such perspective is quite plausible, even valid and necessary to pursue. These accounts can moreover be complemented, if still insufficiently, by corrective studies that attend to Mediterranean culture or to the three monotheistic religions as a unit of one kind or other. Yet one cannot help but wonder at the absence of any consideration, any sustained analysis or even history of "Europe" in its relation to *both* Jew *and* Arab. By suggesting that only the "Jewish question"—and not an "Arab" or "Muslim" one—has been exported by and out of Europe, one forgoes an account of Europe. One naturalizes, moreover, and separates both anti-Semitism and Orientalism in their distinct and anachronistic historical garbs, and, more important, one treats both Jew and Arab as simply existing categories that would have, but for a few exceptions, not to say aberrant instances ("medieval Spain," "Bosnia-Herzegovina"), thoroughly and hermetically distinct histories. There is more at stake here than a straightening of the historical record on Arabs and Jews vis-à-vis or outside of the "Christian West" (Did they really get along? Could they? Why did/do they hate each other? And why do they hate us? Was it peaceful coexistence? What was their true contribution to philosophy, to science, to civilization? And then what happened? And so forth). Nor—does this really need to be said?—is it a matter of asserting that this wrestling match is not of two (or three) parties but of one, that there are no differences or distinctions to be made and maintained. The framing of the question, and, more important, the reflection on its constitutive elements, persists in considering either Jew or Arab and their "place" in Europe independently of each other. Such an approach is not sufficient to account for the current state of affairs, nor does it recognize the ways in which these two political identities—the Jew, the Arab—have been coconstituted by, and most importantly, *with and within*, Europe. The question that must be raised, then, is, Where are the Aryans, the Indo-Europeans? Or what does the Christian want? Or again, and more practically perhaps, What is Europe? What is Europe such that it has managed to distinguish itself from both Jew and Arab (John Paul II once joined Valéry Giscard d'Estaing—along with medieval preachers, inquisitors, ethnic cleansers, and their descendants—by recalling and calling for the Christian identity and integrity of Europe) and to render its role in the theologico-political distinction, in the separation and enmity of Jew *and* Arab invisible—invisible, perhaps most of all to and within "itself"? What, then, of religion and race?

Race and Religion (II)

Arguing for a novel understanding of Shakespeare, Ania Loomba has noted that "ranking somatic, religious or national differences vis-à-vis each other is to continue to think of them as discrete categories."[77] Interestingly enough, although she criticizes this tendency as still operative in the work of scholars such as Julia Reinhard Lupton (who had written that in *Othello* "religious difference is more powerfully felt than racial difference, which was only then beginning to surface in its virulent form"),[78] Loomba does not engage the temporality, nor the historicity, of the distinction that has engaged us here. Nor does she address the overdetermined dimension of highly sedimented disciplinary divisions that, to this day, govern the study of race as distinct from the study of religion. A literary and cultural scholar, Loomba is correct in signaling toward the problematic divide, and she contributes greatly to its undoing. Still, Shakespeare's own text resists, and with it a history that inserts itself, quite precisely, between religion and race. I do not mean, therefore, to criticize Loomba but rather to underscore how complex an understanding of identity-categories her own work—and, by extension, its application to a wider set of issues—demands. Consider, for example, how she describes "the fact that Jews, Moors and Christians were never simply religious categories, but variably articulated with nationality and ethnicity, and often color" (210). Yet, reproducing (or is it prefiguring?) the gesture operative in the invention of the Semites, it is only "the word 'blackamoor'" that, she argues, "collapses religious and somatic vocabularies, which, despite knowledge about white Moors and non-Muslim blacks, could not be unknotted" (211). On the one hand, we cannot maintain the categories as discrete, and on the other hand, they do function together as distinct (if "variably articulated"); finally, on yet another, third, hand, as it were, they only collapse in singular cases. As Loomba points out, "the same writer can make distinctions between the two and collapse them" (211).

Elsewhere, Loomba reminds us that Shakespeare also documents the irreligiosity of the Moor, part of the history I have recalled earlier, whereby Arabs and Saracens were precisely not understood as "having" a religion. Aaron the Moor of *Titus Andronicus* is thus "repeatedly called 'irreligious' and boasts himself that he holds no God sacred," whereas, concerning Othello, "the play [*Othello*] does not comment directly on his religion."[79] Clearly, the histories of Aaron and Othello "illuminate how religion and skin colour intersect in the development of race as a concept" (46). Yet they also underscore the way in which Moors and Muslims, along with the people living in Africa that "were in old time called Aethiopes and Nigritae, which we now call Moores, Moorens, or Negroes," these people, whose religiosity was, in fact, repeatedly denied, were considered to be living "without a God, law, religion, or commonwealth."[80] What Loomba thus uncovers in describing the peculiar intersection of race and religion, in reminding us that "all of Shakespeare's plays that explore the question of race repeatedly return to the question of [religious] conversion of one form or another" (56), is a novel configuration in the process of being fixated. At the time Shakespeare writes, anxieties regarding religious identity are as new, indeed, as modern, as anxieties about racial identity. Or more precisely, anxiety (but much more than an individual mood is here at stake) not only carries with it distinct markers of alterity, but it *produces and manages* them, at times keeping them distant, at times asserting their distinctiveness, at times, finally, collapsing them. As Loomba eloquently puts it, "anxieties about skin colour, religious identity, and female sexuality all overlap; they also all hinge on the relationship between inner and outer being, between what is fixed or natural, and what is artificial and changeable" (63). The Semites—did I mention it?—were female to the Aryan male. One wonders, in spite (and even because) of the insistence on "race, gender, and class," about the continued distinction of academic departments and/or programs: Middle East Studies, Jewish Studies, Women Studies, Religion, Ethnicity, and Race. As with the Jew, the Arab, Israel, and Palestine (the banality of banalization), *separation* never appeared as buttressed. "It does not discern, it discriminates." As did Europe or the West, as they still do. The Semitic hypothesis may constitute a part of the West's now distant past, its "archive of paradise." More likely, though—and what was that word again? That last and worst word?—it remains operative as an "archival record of the unnameable."[81]

2

Secularism

> Note the problem of religion taken not in the confessional sense but in
> the secular sense of a unity of faith between a conception of the world and
> a corresponding norm of conduct. But why call this unity of faith "reli-
> gion" and not "ideology," or even frankly "politics"?
> —Antonio Gramsci, *Prison Notebooks*

> In the chapters that follow, the reader may be certain, however, that as a
> white man I locate myself—all but a painfully extracted sliver of myself—
> *within* the process under scrutiny.
> —Richard Drinnon, *Facing West*

Oppositional Criticism

The alternative appears deceptively simple. It is either the case
that, when using the word *secular*, Edward W. Said did not mean to take
an oppositional stance vis-à-vis religion ("At no point is *secular* used in
his work in simple opposition to the religious per se," explains Aamir
Mufti).[1] Or, insisting on being an *oppositional* critic, he was in fact, and
for a number of elaborate reasons, *against religion.*[2] One could rephrase
the entire matter in milder terms and suggest that the question is whether
Said concerned himself with religion at all, and if he did, how so. Finally,
and whatever formulation and lines of interrogation are adopted, one
could go on to ask whether the term *secular* summarizes or simply ex-
hausts Said's stance (or nonstance) on religion or indeed on the formations of power he thought should be opposed. One may even reach a
conclusion that agrees with those who, like Bruce Robbins, Aamir Mufti,
and others, assert that "the most crucial meaning of *secular*, in [Said's]
usage, is as an opposing term not to religion but to nationalism."[3]

Without retreating from, or immediately adjudicating on, these matters, it is important to acknowledge that within the limited field of academia, a number of critics have learned from Said or taken their point of departure from his work on religion, as it were. In his footsteps they have sought to explore the role and function of religion in the dissemination of colonial knowledge and the founding of institutions (not only in the creation of modern academic discourse and disciplines), in the imperial spread of the secular nation-state, in the making, in short, of what Nicholas Dirks has called "the ethnographic state" and its more recent incarnations.[4] They have also learned from Said when theorizing not only "culture and imperialism" but religion and imperialism, as well, and with it what has been described as the globalization of religion. Whether critical of Said's secularism, here understood as adverse to religion, and which they see as a lingering effect of the very colonial knowledge he criticized; approving "the deployment of 'secular' as an epistemological concept" that has prompted a reexamination of "the roles of secular and religious discourses in both constructing and disputing systems of critical epistemology";[5] or simply ignoring or bracketing Said's own positions (or lack thereof) when arguing about religion and the joined operations of "Orientalism *and* Religion" (as Richard King's book by that title has it), scholars of religion have underscored the growing sense that the discipline of religious studies, though something of a latecomer in engaging some of Said's propositions, has much to learn from his work and from that of his followers. (In the spirit of symmetry, toward which this chapter will incidentally take an oppositional stance, one may wonder whether the reverse is true, whether Said and his followers have any use for religion and religious studies; one may also wonder whether it matters.)

By insisting, however, that Said was *not*—or at least not primarily—concerned with religion when he called for "secular criticism," his less than religiously inclined advocates (or, for that matter, critics) are ignoring a key moment of Said's argument, namely that Orientalism functions *across* disciplines and discourses. In this specific case they keep a reverential distance, showing much deference and respect for disciplinary boundaries that leave religion to scholars of religion, as well as to the interpretive and mobilizing energies of religious communities. They are also repeating what they claim would have been Said's own gesture, namely, one of benign indifference toward religion. ("Above all," explains Mufti, "his concern has been with domination through the classification and management of cultures, and of human collectivities, into mutually distinct and immutable entities, be they nations, properly speaking, or civilizations or ethnicities"—*not* religions.)[6] In the event that, as one may be forgiven for considering somehow more likely, there was nonetheless some negativity toward religion in Said's work and in the work conducted by some of his followers, there would be room legitimately to wonder whether religion, for Said, did not come to function in the way the Orient had for Orientalists. This, at any rate, is William Hart's harsh argument: "if we substitute religion for the Orient, those things to be feared with religious-cultural effects (sacred violence), and those things to be controlled (by quarantine and trivialization), then the irony will be evident. Said Orientalizes religion at the very point that he rescues Islam from Orientalism."[7] Following this familiar logic, and in order to be coherent with his own critique, Said should have extended more respect toward, showed more consideration for, religion. He should have refrained from denigrating it and from advocating secularism, refrained perhaps from being a secularist altogether. He should not have "orientalized" religion. Why? Apparently because reversal could amount to the same thing it opposes on an entirely level playing field (as if Orientalism were "primarily a practice of essentializing, a discursive practice stripped of its entanglement with specific forms and institutions of power in which Orientalist discourse was and remains embedded"),[8] and the kind of hegemony for which the Orientalist was an agent can be reproduced, in the very same terms, by his adversary, the Occidentalist (a well-known professional occupation, I suppose, benefiting from department support and government funding all over the non-Western world, and so forth). Hence Said can be accused of "doing" to religion what the Orientalist "did" to the Orient, which would justify the wagging of impatient fingers at him. And what would those answer who argue that Said did not, in fact, primarily concern himself with religion, who say that religion was not his most crucial adversary? Given the importance of religion today, given, if you will, "the return of the religious" (to be praised or opposed, as if that made a significant difference), they may suggest that religion simply persists as an illusion, an aberrant fossil, the opium of the people or whatnot, and thereby vindicate the fact that Said had little to contribute to a better understanding of this phenomenon's significance—or, indeed, the lack thereof. Everything is as if nothing more needed to be said about religion. Either because religion is not what Said made of it or because the truly important (and somehow surprisingly unrelated) matter is instead secularism. Or, all things being equal again, "culture." Let me already indicate that I do not find these alternatives compelling since I read Said somehow differently.

Clearly, Said's use of the term *secular* was idiosyncratic, although I am not aware of his ever deploying, and certainly not in this particular case, that key phrase of bona fide academic rhetoric, "what I would like to call *x*." If Said *called* or *named* secularism, if he talked about what he allegedly *chose* to call secularism and secular criticism out of some personal commitment, it is first of all because he wished vocally to oppose "secular criticism" to "religious criticism," because he did think and write about religion, about theological and quasi-theological structures and institutions, religious and quasi-religious issues and practices. How idiosyncratic was that? It is hardly a matter of contention that the particular performance that consists in naming anything new or anew is not simply a matter of individual choice or authority, the humanist version of a divine fiat. Jonathan Z. Smith may have argued, in typically polemical fashion, that the word *religion* is a "second-order, generic concept," that it is "a term created by scholars for their intellectual purposes and therefore is theirs to define" (others, again, may try to follow suit by advocating the use of *culture* instead of *religion*), but Said himself never attributed such power to scholars alone.[9] Said made very clear that no matter how significant the lone individual voice is ("Unlike Michel Foucault," Said wrote, "I do believe in the determining imprint of individual writers upon the otherwise anonymous collective body of texts constituting a discursive formation like Orientalism"),[10] it is never the sole or even a privileged source of its own social power nor the ground for its own institutional and political authority. Hence, Julien Benda is "surely wrong . . . to ascribe so much social power to the solitary intellectual whose authority, according to Benda, comes from his individual voice and from his opposition to organized collective passions."[11] The individual is "an isolated voice out of place but very much *of* that place, standing consciously against the prevailing orthodoxy."[12] Being himself "of that place," Said argues against any simple authority or emancipation, against a gesture that would have the individual pull himself up by his bootstraps, as it were, and will himself into a new or autonomous lexicon or private vocabulary, a megajargon, if not a metalanguage. It may be true, therefore, that the word *secular* has "served as a figure for the authority of a putatively universal reason or (narratively speaking) as the ideal endpoint of progress in the intellectual domain."[13] And it is undoubtedly true that forms of authority and domination have changed. Usually, however, or rather, *hegemonically*, the word *secular* has participated in another history and served another function, and with enduring authority. It has operated in a differential relation with, indeed, in opposition to, the word *religious*, doing so within a specific religious tradition (on which more anon), where it had earlier served to mark that which is separated from the sacred or theological. This is so to such an extent that it is not yet possible to argue for any secular position without articulating some understanding of, precisely, religion. Hence, when Talal Asad argues for "an anthropology of the secular," when he claims that the secular is "neither continuous with the religious that supposedly preceded it (that is, it is not the latest phase of a sacred origin) nor a simple break from it," it is emphatically because the *argument* needs to be made, and it needs to be made against "the idea that the secular is a mask for religion, that secular political practices often simulate religious ones," and, finally, because what needs to be shown is that "the 'religious' and the 'secular' are not essentially fixed categories."[14] No one has done more than Asad (and arguably, Said) to show *in the same gesture* the urgency of reflecting on religion and the religious *as well as* on the secular and all its ensuing distinctions. As Said wrote in another context, "from these distinctions," between the religious and the secular, between religion and politics, indeed, from distinctions "which were given their hegemony by the culture, no one could be free."[15]

Covering Religion

Now, when William Hart argues that Said was hostile to religion, that he was in effect "Orientalizing religion," it seems once more that this was Said's personal whim or initiative, a fit of personal inconsistency or creative idiosyncrasy that managed, intentionally or not, to put religion where Orientalists had put the Orient. Here again the power of the sole individual appears momentous and quite arbitrary. So perhaps the question we should ask is how such an apparently arbitrary substitution—of the religious or of the secular—became possible? How did religion come to function in this way for Said (and for others as well)? More precisely, and to be somehow Foucauldean about it, given the quasi-inextricable links that discursively join and disjoin the secular to the religious, how did this configuration imprint its relevance upon the Orient? And vice versa: How did the Orient come to occupy or announce the place of religion? Finally, whence and why is the generic term *religion* shared by Said, by his followers, and by critics alike? Clearly, we are concerned here with particular historical traditions, not just with generic "religions." The "secularized religion" of which Said writes, for example, which was the privileged agent of Orientalism, is after all not just any religion. Nor was it just any "theology" or "culture" (two generic terms that poorly *translate*, that level, the way differences are produced, and the nature of their content). It was Christianity, and more specifically, Western Christendom.

Much more than an idea, Christianity is a massive institution, the sum total of philosophical and scientific, economic and political achievements, discursive, administrative, and institutional accomplishments, the singularity and specificity of which are not to be doubted ("culture and imperialism," "societies for, rather than against, the state," and so forth).[16] Is it not, after all, Christianity that had (and continues to have) a significant and multilayered investment in one particular Oriental city, one particular Oriental land, and one (or two) particular "religions"? And is it not *this* secularized religion—Christianity—that has elaborated and deployed a peculiar discourse *about itself* and *as it understood itself and its history* (in relation to the privileged others to which Said attended), a discourse that consisted in the "critique of religion," that articulated itself as "secular criticism"? To ask this question is not to suggest that "formations of the secular" did not occur in other cultures or that some cultures (or religions—assuming we can effectively differentiate between the two) are incapable of so-called secular progress. Nor is it meant to adjudicate on whether the entire non-Western world is or is not "religious" (who wants to know? And who *translates*? And for what purpose?). Rather, it is to underscore the fact that one particular "religion" is the one whose self-identification with, whose understanding and enforced institutionalization of, that most Latin of words shaped the current, hegemonic use and dissemination of that very same word and its ensuing division of the real, what Jacques Derrida has called *mondialatinisation* and Peter van der Veer "the globalization of Christianity."[17] This one, but complex and, of course, divided, entity has turned against itself, as it were, emancipating itself as if by fiat, by renaming itself "religion" rather than preserving the name it had long given itself as *vera religio*: Christianity.[18] Christianity—what Lynn White has referred to as "our detailed and massive continuity with the European Middle Ages"—is a problematic name, no doubt, but it is a very different generic, because self-ascribed, category.[19] The term, deployed perhaps most efficiently as a target of criticism by Friedrich Nietzsche, is perfectly understandable in its limits and divisions and even more so in its *effects*. It is, at any rate, much less inaccurate historically than the generic *religion*.[20] Christianity it is, then, that actively disenchanted its own world by dividing itself into private and public, politics and economics, indeed, religious and secular.[21] And Christianity turned against itself in a complex and ambivalent series of parallel movements, continuous gestures and rituals, reformist and counterreformist, or revolutionary and not-so-revolutionary upheavals and reversals while slowly coming to name that to which it ultimately claimed to oppose itself: "religion."[22] Munchausen-like, it attempted to liberate itself, to extricate itself from its own conditions: it *judged* itself no longer Christian, no longer "religious." Christianity (that is, to clarify this one last time, Western Christendom) judged and named itself, *reincarnated* itself, as "secular."

It did so—we all know this, of course—at the very moment it was "freeing" itself, spreading its gentle and loving white wings ever further in a world unsuspecting of enchantment or disenchantment, on the heels of earlier missionaries and merchants and by means of the diligent agency of its own "unequal languages" and translators,[23] redemptive missionaries of old and new kinds (self-described Christians all, good or bad, but always faithful and devoted), the diligent agency of its soldiers and other unique scientific achievements. All of these were marvelous possessions, indeed, of the one and only "religion of technology."[24] There were ships, guns, and bombs (later demography and census, airplanes and bigger bombs, and hospitals too, to take care of the wounded) that testified not to technological superiority, as some persistent evolutionism would claim, but to a particular mode—a decision—regarding the usage and deployment of technology.[25] There where, imperial and impervious, it extended itself, Christianity was as unique and worldly as ever (for not every culture practices the Balinese cockfight, perfects the water fountain or the use of medicinal plants, or radically transforms and expands weapons or the institution of slavery). Colonizing the world since 1492, Christianity slowly granted other communities and traditions, those it exploited or converted, massacred and "civilized," enslaved and exterminated, new structures of authority and domination, new and newly negotiable configurations of power. It granted them the name it had only ever attributed to itself, the very name of "religion."[26] It—a complex and even inchoate, often unintentional "it," but one geographically proximate in its origins and governing base, and massively unified across national and denominational boundaries—did all this still in its own name, in the self-avowed name of Christianity, even if not always openly or even knowingly so. Christianity did this, by means of soldiers and missionaries, scholars and politicians, writers and merchants. It, and not just any "religion," not just any "culture," did it all by determining the terms of ensuing negotiations, the terms of discourse, and chief among them was *religion*. Here, then, is where Michel Foucault might help us, with a bit of a gloss, which I provide in brackets in the hope of clarifying that which still ought to make us wonder today:

We are often reminded [but are we really? by whom?] of the countless procedures which Christianity once employed to make us detest the body [and, more recently, religion]; but let us ponder all the ruses that were employed for centuries to make us love [that is, also, hate] sex [and indeed religion], to make the knowledge of it desirable and everything said about it precious. Let us consider the stratagems by which we were induced to apply all our skills to discovering its secrets, by which we were attached to the obligation to draw out its truth, and made guilty for having failed to recognize it for so long. These devices are what ought to make us wonder today.[27]

Following Foucault, then, one would have to reconsider what it might mean today to be "for" or "against" religion, the way Christianity proposed to make its followers into adversaries of the body, the way it made them love some bodies and detest others, as if *free* from the body, and later from religion. Perhaps the awkward, singular logic of this obviously possible but peculiarly unworldly gesture could be highlighted were a community of interpretation to claim, in turn, that they are "against spirit" or, better yet, "against culture" and "against language"? Would it be considered meaningful to be, say, "for politics" and "for economics" but "against knowledge"? Or, as Martin Heidegger taught us, "against technology"? This clever *agencement* of approval or refusal, this rhetoric of freedom as critique—yes, no—about which Nietzsche had much to say, is what Foucault is asking us to consider anew. Following their insight, I propose to take for granted that the religious and the secular are terms that, hopelessly codependent, continue to inform each other and have persisted historically, institutionally, in *masking* (to invoke Asad's term) the one pertinent religion, the one and diverse Christianity and Western Christendom in their transformations and reincarnations, producing the love (or hate) of religion (all scare quotes dropped). Like that unmarked race, which, in the related discourse of racism, became invisible or "white," Christianity invented the distinction between religious and secular, and thus it *made* religion. It made religion the problem—rather than itself. And it made it into an object of criticism that needed to be no less than *transcended*.

The two terms, *religious* and *secular*, are therefore not simply masks for one another. Rather, they function together as strategic devices and as mechanisms of obfuscation and self-blinding, doing so in such a way that it remains difficult, if not impossible, to extricate them from each other as if by fiat. Ultimately, their separation would be detrimental to an analytics of the power of the religious/secular divide, an understanding of its strategic and disciplinary operations. It certainly has been detrimental thus far. Along with the discourse of and on religion (hardly limited to academia, as we know), secularism and secular criticism are unified practices that continue to function the way Christianity has now done for centuries, give or take more or less important differences, complexities, and whatnot. Secularism is part of a discourse of power and of institutions that are bent on making us *invest* "religion," making us *cathect* it (positively or negatively, or even—one can almost see Freud [and Saint Paul] smiling—*indifferently*), bent on making the knowledge of it desirable (or, for that matter, unnecessary), making us know or recognize "religion" for what it is (mostly bad, but others would say, as they did about the Orient, *good*: anti-Semitism and philo-Semitism are never far apart, and "Napoleon tried everywhere to prove that he was fighting *for* Islam"),[28] and mostly, for what it is *not*: Christianity, secularized. Most important, then, secularism is a name Christianity gave itself when it invented "religion," named its other or others as "religions." And the question now is whether there was a specific "religion" that was particularly targeted with this name. Was there one (or two) that was—and may still be—*more* heavily cathected? And if so, which?

It is my contention that in participating in the opposition to religion carried by the terms *secular* and *secularism* (and, let us recognize, Said was unequivocal in arguing against that "curious veering toward the religious" that he was, he claimed, witnessing; in arguing against "this basically uncritical religiosity," discerning "religion as the result of exhaustion, consolation, disappointment" and so forth—as W. J. T. Mitchell pointed out, Said was not really *for* religion, was he?),[29] Said appears simply to have forgotten the lesson taught by this most important of books, namely, *Orientalism*. For if *Orientalism* teaches us anything, it is that Orientalism *is* secularism.

Why? Because *Orientalism* is a critique of Christianity, secularized or not. And Said does clearly point out that as a field of study, "in the Christian West, Orientalism is considered to have commenced its formal existence with the decision of the Church Council of Vienne in 1312 to establish a series of chairs in 'Arabic, Greek, Hebrew, and Syriac at Paris, Bologna, Avignon, and Salamanca.'"[30] And Christianity—which is to say, Orientalism—invented both religion *and* secularism. "With regard to Islam and the Islamic territories, for example, Britain felt that it had legitimate interests, as a Christian power, to safeguard."[31] Christianity invented (or fashioned or produced or enforced, or yet definitely institutionalized by way of knowledge and law—whichever of these you think is better to describe the massive power of hegemony and its operations) Judaism and Islam—the Jew, the Arab, or, to be perfectly historical about it, the Semites—as religions, and more precisely, as being at once *the least and the most religious of religions. And of races.* Subsequently, it cleared the Jews of theological and religious wrongdoings and made Islam the paradigmatic religion, the religion of fanaticism. Doing so, Orientalism—which is to say, secularism—became one of the essential means by which Christianity failed to criticize itself, the means by which Christianity *forgot and forgave* itself.

This endeavor, needless to say, was not a matter of academic politics (and do consider that the disingenuousness of this last remark in the present context does not make it less valid). It was no academic or scholarly matter, nor was it simply a matter of epistemic shifts. It took place as Orientalism "accomplished its self-metamorphosis from a scholarly discourse to an imperial institution," its self-metamorphosis from Christianity to secularism.[32] It took place, as *Orientalism* demonstrates, *across* discourses of knowledge and power: as culture *and* imperialism, as economics *and* politics, and so forth. It still does today.

Said repeatedly, *oppositionally*, pointed to the significance of a ruling elite, which employed or made use of an intellectual elite—often all-too-willing executioners—who together massively created, expanded, sustained, and legitimized a vast structure of political, economic, and cultural domination over the Orient and ultimately over most of the world ("the accommodation between the intellectual class and the new imperialism might very well be accounted one of the special triumphs of Orientalism").[33] Yet Said did not intend thereby to legitimate the enduring activities of the very same—even if new and improved—structures of domination and oppression, which were legitimated by the same institutions (academic, literary, economic, and others) intent on advocating or simply endorsing the continuing domination of suspiciously analogous ruling elites, themselves employing or using (different? more culturally diverse?) intellectual elites (academics or journalists, and today, definitely privileging the latter) and their highly imaginative, collaborative, and distracting abilities. The latter are after all the same elites who, occupying the same places and functions (and a not-altogether-different dress code), were and remain devoted, wittingly or not, to the training and exercise of the power of the few over the millions, indeed, billions of individuals conveniently located in the very same neighborhoods, the very same areas of the world colonized and administered, massively transformed by good and bad Christians since 1492 (national and denominational distinctions being, of course, essential to uphold in order to deny the hegemonic unity of a joined, if also divisive and divided, lasting endeavor). Like Nietzsche, Said was oppositional to the extent that he was only attacking victorious causes. And—is this really news?—secularism *is* a victorious cause. It participates in a set of devices that make "religion" (the religion of the others, that is, or their nationalism, or what have you) more of an ominous danger than, say, the dealings of the ruling and no longer welfare states, the practices of gigantic corporations and their national and international backing, to say nothing of homeland security and its consequences. Secularism—internal *and* external colonialism—is produced and reproduced by way of law and rhetoric, national and international institutions, chief among them the modern states, hardly declining commercial and security apparatuses. Secularism continues to be fostered by the same institutions, and structurally identical elites, out of the same centers of power that earlier spread their "civilization" and continue to expand their mission, be it economic, military, cultural, or whatever. It still has the bigger bombs—it *is* the history of bombing—and the bigger police, security, military, and financial forces.[34] It builds the bigger walls. Minimally, it maintains its hold on the institutions that preserve and reproduce a power structure and a ruling and intellectual elite that suffers or holds with true *Gelassenheit* (and a few international laws and trade agreements) those billions in abject poverty, judging unsatisfactory their inability to escape the dark theological ages out of the depth of which they seek artificial comfort and solace. There would be the problem, along with the demonstration of the poor man's and woman's inability to restrain their theological or quasi-theological and whatever other "religious" failings.

Thus to uphold *secularism* (or, for that matter, religion) as the key word for critical endeavors and projects today is, I am afraid, not to be that worldly. It is to oppose the world rather than that which makes and unmakes it as what it is not (or at least not yet). It is to oppose the world and those who inhabit it rather than those who make it unlivable. It is, at any rate, certainly not to deal with "local and worldly situations," if by that one means the world populated by the oppressed (and by a perfectly "secular" play of market forces gently trickling down on them), those all too often considered to have no "critical distance" vis-à-vis their own lives, "archaic" ideals, and, indeed, worlds. Indeed, how could "religion" ever be considered otherworldly? How could otherworldliness ever be considered otherworldly? In what world? As being-in-the-world, religion is not inequality. Inequality is. Religion cannot be willed out of worldly existence by secularists who deny its "fictional" or oppressive escape while affirming the cultural and political importance of that other fictive production based on infinite credit and credulousness: literature—or was it the market? To uphold secularism today is to erase the fact that secularism continues to serve inequality. It serves mostly—and certainly has *historically* served—one particular religion (the missionizing activities of which have anything but slowed down, by way of "secular institutions of higher learning," the pope, or other corporations or, if there is a difference, those megachurches), and one economic game, one elite-serving apparatus, namely, the secular nation-state (and the corporations to which, Hannah Arendt was already reminding us, it continues to cater), the discourse of power that legitimates itself and presents itself as secular, as if *indifferent* to religion yet *producing religion as a (generic) problem.* Secularism's key words—consensual key words for one key word among others—are *human rights, international law, sovereignty, democracy,* and so forth, all of which are avowedly "secular" projects that have yet to achieve equality. Is it possible to be for or against these? However reductive this might be, it is not difficult to see that these words are the new or resuscitated names of a not-so-new civilizing mission, and they work in tandem with the negated binary terms they seek to oppose or repress (but in fact *produce,* as Foucault taught us). It is not so much that Said's words on religion recall the Orientalists' Orient. Rather, religion is the Orient. That is why it is possible to quote Said and substitute *religion* for *the Orient*: "As momentous, generally important issues face the world— issues involving nuclear destruction, catastrophically scarce resources, unprecedented human demands for equality, justice, and economic parity—popular caricatures of [religion] are exploited by politicians whose source of ideological supply is not only the half-literate technocrat but the superliterate Orientalist."[35]

What does secularism make us hate, then? Racism, nationalism, sexual inequalities, and, all right, religion. But whose religion? And where? And who advocates secularism? Who opposes racism, nationalism, sexual inequalities, and religion, and from where? With what effects? What are the geopolitics of that "struggle for justice," the struggle against the oppression of women and, yes, against anti-Semitism? Said's own key words—*Orientalism, Imperialism, Secularism*—may not be so different from each other after all ("Long ignored as an object of Said's scholarship, in favor of the concept of Orientalism or the rubric of culture and imperialism, this term [i.e., *secularism*] and its significations are now coming to be seen as a constellation that animates Said's critical practice as a whole").[36] To repeat then: Secularism is Orientalism. And Orientalism is Christianity. It is Christian Imperialism. Edward Said knew it too (as I will attempt to show in the remainder of this chapter), by which I mean that he *demonstrated* it. Only he forgot that he had; he forgot that he had written the book on it, a book dedicated, as it were, to religion.

Orientalism: A Critique of Christianity

> In fact, you cannot be a philologist or doctor without being *anti-Christian* at the same time.
> —Friedrich Nietzsche, *The Anti-Christ*

So, what in the world is religion? For purposes of expediency and clarity, I will base my answer on *Orientalism* because the "Semitic Orient" still holds a special place, a paradigmatic one, in relation to other, even if sometimes more fatally loved, colonized and missionized areas— and Melville's "metaphysics of Indian-hating," among others, does come to mind here.[37] *Orientalism* reveals that religion is a discursive device that enables the workings of power (or, in Timothy Fitzgerald's more contained formulation, "'religion' derives its plausibility and apologetics as a generally viable analytical category, in the face of a mass of contradictory evidence, from its mystifying function in western liberal capitalist ideology").[38] So much for a news flash—but this was 1979 and "the return of the religious" (read, the Iranian revolution) had yet to become obvious to most observers. The device operates in such a way that the key distinctions it produces or participates in producing, whether epistemologically, politically, or legally, are made to disappear and reappear in tune with their strategic usefulness. One key distinction is, of course, the distinction between religious and secular (as in "we" are secular, "they" are religious). Another is that between nationalism and religion. Underscoring or advocating one term means "forgetting" or indeed masking the other. (Is it possible not to notice—in spite of Azmi Bishara's tireless efforts to remind us—that American foreign policy, like its British, French, and other seasoned and enduring fellow travelers, has long been intent on strategically playing Islam against Arab nationalism, ethnicity against religion, and local nationalism against religious unity? Is it possible not to notice that religion and nationalism are strategically divided and must therefore be considered in their joined operations?) Hence, the secularization of religion, for someone like Ernest Renan, who was "determined to be as Christian as he once was, only now without Christianity and with what he called 'la science laïque' (secular science),"[39] is the condition for the rise of nationalism. The separation, the transcending of particularity, whether race or religion, is done in the name of a new universal, namely, the nation. The move from particular to universal, that paradigmatically Christian trajectory, should not jar in a writer as Christian or post-Christian (or whatever) as Renan or Comte and countless others. Said made this perfectly clear: "No less than Schlegel, Wordsworth, and Chateaubriand, Auguste Comte—like [Flaubert's] Bouvard—was the adherent and proponent of a secular post-Enlightenment myth whose outlines are unmistakably Christian."[40] Another key distinction, subsumed under the nation for Renan and others, but one more directly engaged in *Orientalism*, is that between race and religion. Indeed, with the rise of secular science, "race, color, origin, temperament, character, and types overwhelmed *the distinction between Christians and everyone else*" (120; emphasis added). Thus, it is not simply that "the old religious patterns of human history and destiny and 'the existential paradigms'" were "reconstituted, redeployed, redistributed in the secular frameworks." It is not simply the case that what "Orientalism *did* and what Orientalism *was*" consisted in the retention of "an undislodged current in its discourse, a reconstructed religious impulse, a naturalized supernaturalism" (121). It is not simply the case because that particular "religious impulse" did not originate in just any "religion." It was not the substitute or offspring of just any past history. Rather, "the essential aspects of modern Orientalist theory and praxis (from which present-day Orientalism derives) can be understood not as a sudden access of objective knowledge about the Orient but as a set of structures inherited from the past, secularized, redisposed, and re-formed by such disciplines as philology, which in turn were naturalized, modernized, and laicized substitutes for (or versions of) *Christian supernaturalism*" (122; emphasis added).

Does this all mean that Said (or at least my reading of Said) denies agency to non-Christians, attributing it only to an all-powerful, determining Christianity? Absolutely not. Yet before rushing to all-too-common counterfactual arguments about the equal-opportunity devastation *potentially* unleashed by *all* cultures if they only had the chance, Said elaborates a theory of agency that permits dwelling on historical occurrences, on the actual deployment of power in its specific modes and strategies. And its effects. We have seen that Said draws our attention once again to the fact that the scholar (or the individual) does not create his or her own language. Doing so, Said underscores what the increased usage of the word *agency* in academic discourse has tended to ignore, namely, one of the major semantic dimensions of that word. Said does so when he suggests that "the Orientalist could be regarded as the special agent of Western power as it attempted policy vis-à-vis the Orient." In some cases, the Orientalist could even perform his role "as a kind of secret agent *inside* the Orient."[41] The scholar, indeed, the intellectual class in the Orient, as well as *of* the Orient, indeed, the Orient "itself," can all be understood as agents, double agents, even, and therefore as having agency. But the operations of such agencies function across disciplines and discourses, between knowledge and power, without respecting the Weberian notion of the modern separation of spheres. The equally divided agency that is Orientalism, such that it persists in its being, pursues and fosters the case of religion (or of secularism, for that matter) in ways that have remained insufficiently explored. "That is why questions about what it is possible for agents to do must also address the process by which 'normal persons' are constituted."[42] But there are many agencies, other than the individual, although this too, along with its operations, remains understudied (in Partha Chatterjee's terms, one could say that we do not have, but perhaps desperately need, "a Kalabari anthropology of the white man" no less than we need to confront the difficulties involved in "an anthropological description of Christianity").[43] This network of agencies, of Christian agencies that produce and institutionalize the division between religious and secular, constitute, to my mind, one of the cores of Said's argument. And it is one that was difficult to keep in mind. Even for Said himself.

Said did not make it easy on his readers, but rather than fault him, we should probably admire the fact that he was working against all odds. As I have already suggested, Christianity made itself increasingly forgettable by foregrounding "religion" as a generic category and a target of criticism (and look today at all the smart bombs aimed at a generic and leveled "monotheism"), doing so at the same time that it was arguing for the end of religion in its own practice, often pushing its colonial endeavor as a kind of critical secularism, a secular science.[44] No wonder, then, that religion seems mostly absent from Said's own pathbreaking account of the operations of Orientalism. Indeed, as "a style of thought" Orientalism drafted into its service "a very large mass of writers, among whom are poets, novelists, philosophers, political theorists, economists, and imperial administrators" but apparently neither priests nor theologians, no religious scholars nor missionaries.[45] And what these free agents, these secular agents, diligently produced were "elaborate theories, epics, novels, social descriptions, and political accounts," but no religious accounts. They produced "the Orient politically, sociologically, militarily, ideologically, scientifically, and imaginatively" (3); they "designated Asia or the East, geographically, morally, culturally" (31) but not, or so it would seem, religiously. Certainly, "the scientist, the scholar, the missionary, the trader, or the soldier" all had a collective hand in this production (7). They all had a hand in the emergence of the Orient, but the religious relevance or dimension of that hand and its products appears almost marginal, an afterthought: "There emerged a complex Orient suitable for study in the academy, for display in the museum, for reconstruction in the colonial office, for theoretical illustration in anthropological, biological, linguistic, racial, and historical theses about mankind and the universe, for instances of economic and sociological theories of development, revolution, cultural personality, national or religious character" (8–9). This conspicuously marginal, almost belated status of the religious would explain why Orientalism functions as "a *distribution* of geopolitical awareness into aesthetic, scholarly, economic, sociological, historical, and philological texts," why it deploys a series of "interests" by means of "scholarly discovery, philological reconstruction, psychological analysis, landscape and sociological description" (12). "Indeed, the very project of restriction and restructuring associated with Orientalism can be traced directly to the inequality by which the Orient's comparative poverty (or wealth) besought scholarly, scientific treatment of the kind to be found in disciplines like philology, biology, history, anthropology, philosophy, or economics" (150). It would explain why the "distinctive differences" at stake are "differences between races, civilizations, and languages" (233), with religion nowhere to be found.

Or perhaps, unreadable, invisible in its magnitude, religion is everywhere. After all, "can one divide human reality, *as indeed human reality seems to be genuinely divided*, into clearly different cultures, histories, traditions, societies, even races, and survive the consequences humanly?" (45). Do we not need to ask, therefore, "what other sorts of intellectual, aesthetic, scholarly, and cultural energies went into the making of the imperialist tradition like the Orientalist one? How did philology, lexicography, history, biology, political and economic theory, novel-writing and lyric poetry come to the service of Orientalism's broadly imperialist view of the world?" (15). If, "as historians of science and knowledge have observed, the organization of scientific and learned fields that took place during the nineteenth century was both rigorous and all encompassing" (191), what of the field of religion? What of its force field? Is it not the case, in other words, that if we can (as indeed we must) treat "the cultural, historical phenomenon of Orientalism as a kind of *willed human work*," it may ultimately be because it has everything to do with a particular form of will and works, indeed, with "faith and works"?

In the early history of the Orient's making, Said explains very clearly, "Christianity completed the setting up of the main intra-Oriental spheres: there was a Near Orient and a Far Orient" (58). The secure distance at which even the *near* Orient could be held by Western Christianity quickly vanished, however, as Islam came much closer, prior to the Crusades that enabled its being reframed as *distant*, and so to this day. Islam was *in* Europe (it still is: "the Orient and Islam are always represented as outsiders having a special role to play *inside* Europe" [71], in marked contrast with, say, India, which "never provided an indigenous threat to Europe" [75]), and it evoked mainly fear and terror. Christian Europe, or in Said's own words "Christianity," "Christians," and "Christian authors," responded to Islam "with very little except fear and a kind of awe" (59). For Europe, then, for Christian Europe, "Islam was a lasting trauma" (ibid.), a painful and extended thorn in the "universal and eternal system of Christian values" (68). This is why Islam is not simply an arbitrary moment chosen by Said for reasons of "personal investment" (25). Rather, Islam is the key figure in the making of the Orient (and hence the Occident), indeed, a paradigmatic one. "The European encounter with the Orient, and specifically with Islam . . . turned Islam into the very epitome of an outsider against which the whole of European civilization from the Middle Ages on was founded" (70). And so, "given its special relationship to both Christianity and Judaism, Islam remained forever the Orientalist's idea (or type) of *original* cultural effrontery, aggravated naturally by the fear that Islamic civilization originally (as well as contemporaneously) continued to stand somehow opposed to the Christian West" (260). No Orientalism without Christianity, nor without Islam (or Judaism). But is Islam a religion?

It is quite striking to consider that, when reading *Orientalism*, the answer to this question is far from obvious. When describing the early Christian responses to Islam, Said emphasizes that it appears "a radically new form of life," a "raw novelty," and, more negatively, "a fraudulent new version of some previous experience, in this case Christianity" (59). Said knows well that Islam was often considered a heresy and that this was more or less the full extent of its theological content, if it had any. Over that early encounter, there undoubtedly emerged a "rigorous Christian picture of Islam" (61), and it is from that picture, it seems, from that Christian picture, that Europe embarked on its Oriental journey. Having started with Islam, "it is as if, having once settled on the Orient as a locale suitable for incarnating the infinite in a finite shape, Europe could not stop the practice" (62). The Christian theological dimension of Orientalism, and the way it has honed itself on Islam as a privileged object from its earliest stages, can hardly be doubted. But this does not mean that Islam is understood as a religion. In fact, the 1697 *Bibliothèque orientale* by Barthélemy d'Herbelot states quite explicitly that Muslims *claim the name of religion*, something to which they have in fact no right ("This is the famous imposter Mahomet, Author and Founder of a heresy, *which has taken on the name of religion*, which we call Mohammedan" [quoted on 66; emphasis added]). In 1787 the Comte de Volney publishes his *Voyage en Égypte et en Syrie*, "an almost oppressively impersonal document," the climax of which "occurs in the second volume, *an account of Islam as a religion*" (81; emphasis added). Or recall Caussin de Perceval's 1847 thesis "that the Arabs were made a people by Mohammed, Islam being essentially a political instrument, not by any means a spiritual one" (151). Islam would be "an exclusively political movement," void of any religious force (152). Finally, in 1931, the German Orientalist Carl Becker still felt the urge to argue that "to understand Islam one needed above all else to see it, not as an 'original' religion, but as a sort of failed Oriental attempt to employ Greek philosophy without the creative inspiration that we find in Renaissance Europe" (104). Hence, Said rightly comments on this enduring, if waning, Christian perspective that far from being a religion, Islam would have been an "imitation of a Christian imitation of *true religion*" (66; emphasis added). This is how "the Orient is accommodated to the moral exigencies of Western Christianity," how the Orient is shaped as an event within the history of religion (as nonreligion) and later as paradigmatically religious (with variations on the theme: "to some of the German Romantics, for example, Indian religion was essentially an Oriental version of the Germano-Christian pantheism" [67]). Not until the nineteenth century does the division so neatly marked (and undone) today between a secular West and a "mystic East" (as Richard King recalls) come to establish itself so forcefully. Edgar Quinet may have put it most succinctly when he wrote in his 1832 *Le génie des religions*: "L'Asie a les prophètes, l'Europe a les docteurs" (quoted on 79). But the phenomenon reaches much wider, here too, than Quinet's own peculiar view. The series of transformations whereby Islam could *become* a religion, rather than be released "from the narrowly religious scrutiny by which it had hitherto been examined (and judged) by the Christian West" (120), was a general one and included Napoleon's identification with Muslims ("Nous sommes les vrais musulmans," he proclaimed in 1798), his conviction that "he was fighting *for* Islam" and his apparently "obvious veneration for the Koran" (82). Positive or negative (and for scholars like Goldziher, Massignon, and Gibb, it was overwhelmingly, even if not exclusively, positive), Islam is at the center of the Orientalist imagination. That it is not alone there does not diminish its paradigmatic value. On the contrary. For whether understood, as Said never tired of explaining, as the twin image of the Jew in the anti-Semitic imagination, or as the paradigmatic Semitic figure in its opposition to the Aryan, Islam remains the main target of Orientalist schemes. It is that which must, but perhaps cannot, be understood, the privileged site of an endless enterprise of explanation and preoccupation. More important, it is the target of all efforts of what Said calls the "secularized religion" of Orientalism.

From the "promotion of Christian knowledge" and the continuous, if more aleatory, missionary activities of the British and French empires, the "reconstituted theology" and "natural supernaturalism" of the eighteenth century (114), and the claim by the German Romantics that "it was Indian culture and religion that could defeat the materialism and mechanism (and republicanism) of Occidental culture" (115); from the "borders of Christian Europe" that "no longer served as a kind of custom house" (120) to "the reconstructed religious impulse" of Orientalism as a whole, and to the Orientalist's celebration of "his method, and his position, as that of a secular creator, a man who made new worlds as God had once made the old" (121), the subjects of Orientalism are "unmistakably Christian" (115), but they are also mourning—or celebrating—the loss of their religion. "In other words, modern Orientalism derives from the secularizing elements in eighteenth-century European culture" (120). Which is to say that with the invention of new, comparative disciplines ("philology, anatomy, jurisprudence, religion" [117]), Europe is discovering its own gods to be part of a much larger pantheon. It is discovering anew the old languages it can now classify in novel fashion, Aryan versus Semite. Indeed, "Arabic and Hebrew are Semitic languages, and together they dispose and redispose the material that is urgently important to Christianity" (74). It is at this point—and at this point only—that Christianity can become one among many "religions" rather than the

Church confronting Jews, Muslims, and other heretics. Said delves into the details of such transformation, the completion and achievement of Christianity—Renan and others might say its *aryanization* too—in and through science, in and through Orientalism, such as it occurs in de Sacy ("he acted in his writing like a secularized ecclesiastic for whom his Orient and his students were doctrine and parishioners respectively" [124]) and Renan (who "assimilated himself to philology according to his own post-Christian fashion" [135], whose "study of Semitic [was] replacing his faith" [140]). But, more important, Said demonstrates that Orientalism is an enterprise that produces rather than reproduces religion, a general attempt by Orientalists "radically to recast into terms appropriate to the historical and intellectual circumstances of their own age, the Christian pattern of the fall, the redemption, and the emergence of a new earth which will constitute a restored paradise" (138, quoting Renan). Where Christianity was, there is now religion, and this makes all the difference.

Consider the titles of the works Said highlights. Whereas earlier Orientalists focus on travel and the discovery of the strange and foreign (Edward William Lane is still operating under this older regime of "pilgrims and pilgrimages," studying "manners and customs"), nineteenth-century Orientalists install the foundations of modern knowledge. Before sociology and anthropology, before literature even, there was the Orient as religion. Indeed, these Orientalists were quickly on their way to becoming experts on nothing but religion, creating in fact the very field of comparative religion and religious studies (Max Müller, Renan) as they make or unmake "religions." Among "the innumerable Orientalist texts on Islam" (109), it is therefore imperative to consider the founding texts of the modern making—the modern *covering* (to invoke another of Said's works)—of "religion": Quinet, *Le génie des religions* (a "key text" and "a work that announced the Oriental Renaissance and placed the Orient and the West in a functional relationship with each other" [137]); Constant, *De la religion*; Robertson Smith, *The Religion of the Semites*; Duncan MacDonald, *The Religious Attitude and Life in Islam*; and so forth. At stake is the repetitive power of a magisterial demonstration intent on arguing and showing that "the Semites are rabid monotheists who produced no mythology, no art, no commerce, no civilization" (142, quoting Renan), sedimenting that which had hardly been obvious earlier, namely that Islam is, in fact, "a living and vital religion" (281, quoting Gibbs). Semites—that is Muslims and Jews, but soon no longer the Jews—are nothing but a religion, the best and the worst of it.

And what, again, is a religion? First of all, it is something that, essential to the Orientalist vision, "could be studied apart from the economics, sociology and politics of the Islamic people" (105). "History, politics, and economics do not matter. Islam is Islam, the Orient is the Orient" (107). Before the work of Durkheim and other sociologists and anthropologists of religion, there was the work of Orientalism. It formulated the notion that a religion is not a nation, something that produced an insistence on the religious dimension of the Orient—and primarily, urgently, of Islam. This had the effect, in turn, of diminishing, even erasing, the political dimension of Islam (and vice versa, as we have seen). That is why Arab or Islamic nationalism is said to be anything but political, why it is anything but nationalism, why it "lacks, in spite of its occasional use as a catchword, the concept of the divine right of a nation, it lacks a formative ethic, it also lacks, it would seem, the later nineteenth century belief in mechanistic progress" (297, quoting von Grunebaum). Finally, a religion, that is to say, Islam as religion, is the quintessential enemy of secular civilization: "the sword of Muhammed, and the Kor'an, are the most stubborn enemies of Civilization, Liberty, and the Truth which the world has yet known" (151, quoting Dozy). One could thus conceive without difficulty of the following analogy: that Islam is to Europe what "religious criticism" is to "secular criticism," what "religion" is to "secularism."

"My contention," Said says, "is that Orientalism is fundamentally a *political* doctrine willed over the Orient because the Orient was weaker than the West, which elided the Orient's difference with its weakness" (204; emphasis added). What Said says is right, of course, and he makes clear that nationalism, Arab nationalism in particular, was always a major target of Orientalist ire. What Said does, however, is show that essential to an understanding of that East/West difference is the transformation of both East and West into "religions," the transformation of Orientalism as Western Christendom into Orientalism as secularism (that is as a new and improved, reformed and secularized, Western Christendom). But this is no simple transformation, not a new and *equal* division of the world into religious entities. Rather, covering Islam means covering religion, making and masking it.

Now, it is true that, as Tomoko Masuzawa has compellingly shown, Europe came to a distinct kind of self-consciousness through these operations. Whereas "for many centuries Europeans had a well-established convention for categorizing the people of the world into four parts, rather unequal in size and uneven in specificity, namely, Christians, Jews, Mohammedans (as Muslims were commonly called then), and the rest," what came to pass in the course of the transformation Said so cogently describes is that "this conventional ordering began to lose its ruling authority." Instead, argues Masuzawa, "there suddenly appeared an entirely new system, namely, a list of roughly ten to a dozen 'world religions.'"[46] Like Said, Masuzawa underscores the peculiar status of Islam in the Orientalist, Christian, or secular perspective. In it Islam oscillates between its complete lack of theological validity and a paradigmatic, extreme, religious fanaticism. But what Said uniquely shows is that the category of religion (albeit invisible at times) is part of a much larger apparatus that functions *across* Weberian divisions. It cannot therefore be reduced to "the religious" or to "religions" but must include rather a wider logic of contemporary, discriminating separations and divisions into nations, races, and cultures (as well as sexual difference, as Said also underscores). It is the demonstration of the full extent of this complex and internally divided, highly hierarchical apparatus as it emerges from the Christian West, the power of which Said's *Orientalism* demonstrates and opposes. That is why Orientalism is no mere *political* doctrine (although it is that too); it is also a *religious* one (and, to be sure, an economic and scientific one). To be more precise, before Claude Lefort asked about a "permanence of the theologico-political," Said demonstrated the persistence of Christianity as a singular deployment of that division in its multiple configurations, at once "religious" and "secular." That is why *Orientalism* is a critique of Christianity and also why, if accessorily and marginally so, it is an essential work for the study of religion (not just of religious studies), that is to say, for an understanding of the global division between religious and secular (religion and race, religion and nationalism, religion and politics, and so forth). Had Said recognized his own momentous accomplishment, he would have had to acknowledge that his work was indeed critical of religion but that it was also, and for reasons of hegemony perhaps more profoundly, opposed to secularism. More precisely, though, Said could have refrained from being for or against religion, for or against secularism. Instead, and in true Nietzschean fashion, Said would have had to become what he already was. He would have had to be—how is this for oppositional criticism?—anti-Christian.

PART II

LITERATURE

Literary History and Hebrew Modernity

> Assertions of literary modernity often end up by putting the possibility of
> being modern seriously into question.
> —Paul de Man, "Literary History and Literary Modernity"

To write reflectively about Hebrew literature means to acknowledge
its modernity. Yet, more than the usefulness of the term *modernity*, it is
perhaps its efficacy that leads to difficulty. Acknowledging the conflict
between history and modernity, while embodying an ethos of literary
history, Hebrew literature has sought to describe, assert, or establish its
singularity. This endeavor, which may remain implicit in literary practice,
must and has become explicit in critical practice. As the problematic unity
of sets of practices, and with varying degrees of self-consciousness, the
whole of Hebrew literature takes part in the production of separations,
distinctions, and determinations that touch on history and periodization,
genre and movements, legacy and rebellion, center and margin, inside
and outside, and more. It is, no doubt, an effect of increased self-consciousness that such distinctions have multiplied and that critics have
been involved in sharpening them. Writers and critics have thus engaged
in what may appear as a "narcissism of minor differences" but could be
more accurately described as a search for the new, "a genuine impulse
toward modernity," seeking to define the new, to recognize or produce it.[1]
This desire for the new explains, if only partly, why the privileged site of
contemporary Hebrew literature is modernity (and, within it, modernism) and its limits. The sheer novelty of the forms and kinds of Hebrew
writing such as began in Europe two hundred years ago and the repeated

attempt to determine the nature of that critical—that is, decisive, distinguishing, separating—moment is therefore paradigmatic of the way in which Hebrew literature seeks to determine its singularity. Accounting for the new and for singularity has been and remains the privileged and crucial task of literary critics across national boundaries, prominent among them literary historians. Accordingly, and because the concern with the new appears quintessentially modern, most histories of Hebrew literature are not only modern (in the historical sense of belonging to modernity), but they primarily attend to a modern phenomenon, namely, Modern Hebrew literature. Thus, "the term 'modernity' reappears with increasing frequency and seems again to have become an issue not only as an ideological weapon, but as a theoretical problem as well" (142).

Clearly, "a desire to wipe out whatever came earlier, in the hope of reaching at last a point that could be called a true present, a point of origin that marks a new departure" can be found in various forms in a number of, and perhaps in all, literary traditions.[2] "The appeal of modernity," in other words, "haunts all literature."[3] The desire for a clean break is part and parcel of the constitution and institution of *national* literary traditions. It partakes of an act of critical judgment directed toward and against the literary self, individual or collective. It embodies, finally, the undoing of the inclusive and exclusive boundaries of the literary object. But this desire also acquires a particular poignancy in situations of bilingualism (or of polylingualism), in diasporic or migrant settings, or in colonial and postcolonial conditions. In most of these cases the conflict of distinctions, beginning with the opposition between tradition and modernity, takes place by means of a name that often appears to erase differences at the very moment it buttresses others ("women's literature," "Chinese literature"). Or it is emblematized by a new name (one that is often no less hegemonic and difference-erasing but marks, nonetheless, a recognizable site of difference, for better or for worse).[4] Here one could think of any number of proliferating linguistic markers that have thankfully, if often problematically, come to function as alternatives to the labels and confines of national literatures ("Anglophone," as opposed to English; "Francophone," as opposed to French; and so forth).[5] What has been most forcefully demonstrated thereby is less an acknowledgment of singularity, less a refashioning of literariness, than, no doubt, that, over against literature "itself," "what we usually call literary history has little or nothing to do with literature."[6] More broadly and more important, these institutional developments have confirmed that "the bases for historical knowledge are not empirical facts but written texts, even if these texts masquerade in the guise of wars or revolutions" (165). Nowhere is this more evident today than in the case of Hebrew literature, where for some time now wars have masqueraded in the guise of texts.[7]

What follows is an attempt to engage the singularity of Hebrew literature, its modernity as "ideological weapon" in the critical and institutional wars it has conducted with its outside as well as with itself. Beginning with the question of language (or languages, as Yitzhak Laor paradoxically suggests), "Hebrew literature inherited a rift between its cultural and spoken languages that it has been unable to repair."[8] This rift is, in a sense, at the basis of a war that "has little or nothing to do with literature." Indeed, while the participation (one might say, the collaboration and, at rare times, the critique) of Hebrew literature in the wars of Israel against Palestine has long been recognized—most sharply perhaps by Laor himself, who aptly described Israeli literature as the production of "narratives with no natives," thus highlighting that there are other, more covert, wars—it is unclear what the stakes are in approaching intellectual or academic developments in literary studies in the United States (but elsewhere, too, and always far from Israeli state apparatuses, at least apparently) as if they were today an urgent or even a determining moment of these wars.[9] Yet stakes there appear to be when, following more than thirty years of unprecedented and uninterrupted growth of programs, centers, or departments of Jewish Studies, and the more recent explosion of Holocaust studies within or without these same structures, we are now witnessing the mushrooming of more programs and centers, this time of Israel studies.[10] What is coming under scrutiny, if hardly gaining clarity, is not only a wide range of "ideological weapons" but, more important, the highly contested nature—to say the least—of the distinction between Jewish and Israeli, between Zionist and Jew, and, in a different register, between Hebrew and Jewish. At the juncture between critical and institutional thinking, Hebrew literature has already staked much in this last distinction.[11] Strangely enough, it has also succeeded in erasing its manifest relevance by sealing the hegemony of Hebrew.

Writing in 1962, Arnold Band, today still one of the leading American critics of Hebrew literature, could already dedicate the bulk of a lecture on "Jewish Literature in the University" to Hebrew literature. Acknowledging, for example, that "modern Hebrew writers comprised a determined and talented minority that never commanded a vast audience until the last generation or two," acknowledging as well that the close relations between Yiddish literature and Hebrew literature are historically fraught ("after all, most Hebrew and Yiddish writers between 1860 and 1920 wrote in both languages") and have remained understudied in spite of the obvious closeness ("we still don't have a history of literature which presents an adequate statement of the peculiar relationship between the two literatures"), Band presents "Hebrew or Jewish literature" as if it constituted one term, at best two equivalent terms, that cover the same unified area of cultural production.[12] "Hebrew or Jewish literature," he writes, lamenting what was once a rare or marginal curricular offering, "is not the only area of cultural importance missing from the curriculum of most American universities, but the exclusion of Jewish literature . . . cannot be attributed either to geographical distance from Europe or the humanistic insignificance of the values embodied in it" (384). The unified area of cultural importance here ostensibly described in the singular appears, furthermore, to cover the same geographical area, the same "values" as Europe. But be that as it may, the question remains of the distinction nonetheless made, be it syntactically, and at other times, historically (there are "periods" and "centers" of Jewish literature, but there is also—and the status of this "also" locates the entire question we are engaging—"modern Hebrew literature," even if "we don't even have a label in English for the specialist in post-Biblical Jewish literature" [372]). More recently, Dan Miron, the foremost Israeli critic of Modern Hebrew (and Yiddish) literature could assert, on the basis of his assessment of a past and present, allegedly unified, "national culture," that "there is no such thing as a unified Jewish literature, and there has not been one since the fragmentation of our national culture at the end of the eighteenth and beginning of the nineteenth centuries."[13] Clearly, Hebrew ("our national culture") and Jewish are not one and the same. How, then, does Hebrew literature intervene in the construction (or destruction) of Jewish literature? How does Modern Hebrew literature configure its past and its present in relation to Jewish literature (or Jewish literatures)?

Between Histories

The history of Hebrew literature as part of the practice of Hebrew literature is thus essentially modern: it is the modern history of Hebrew literature and it is the history of Modern Hebrew literature. This is empirically true (the overwhelming majority of books of Hebrew literary history are histories of Modern Hebrew literature or chapters thereof), but it also partakes of a more abstract, modern phenomenon whereby the self-conscious concern with history and with the new have themselves become determining. The distinction, the quarrel even, between "les anciens et les modernes" must itself be "modern" (in a relative sense), and it takes greater urgency with the new historical task that seeks to define modernity, that takes it upon itself to define the distinct nature of its own modernity, as well as the modernity of its object. Thus, "modernity turns out to be indeed one of the concepts by means of which the distinctive nature of literature can be revealed in all its intricacy."[14]

Commenting on the elusive singularity of Modern Hebrew literature, its most prominent critics have embraced the term along with its highly discriminating objective. Works with titles such as *Modern Hebrew Literature, Modern Hebrew Fiction, Hebrew and Modernity* are proliferating and too numerous to list, whether in Hebrew or in English. In some cases, leaving out the term *modern* functions to reinscribe its force, as well as the critical intent behind it, "the hope of reaching at last a point that could be called a true present, a point of origin that marks a new departure," as de Man put it. Thus, Gershon Shaked, whose major contribution has been to diagnose a kind of modernity within modernity, a "new wave" in Israeli fiction (one that would be described from "as present, as contemporary a perspective as possible, *mi-nequdat re'ut 'akhshavit ke-khol ha-efshar*"), documents the development of "Hebrew fiction" beginning in the 1880s.[15] Here modernity remains implicit. It is simply assumed at the precise moment that demonstrating its historical distinctiveness remains the goal to achieve. Shaked writes, "Hebrew fiction has its own internal development, and in order to determine its distinctiveness, one must separate it from its parallels [lit. "sisters, *ahayiot*"] and attend to its history on its own."[16] Earlier, Dov Sadan had done extensive work to address the numerous difficulties involved in writing a history of Modern Hebrew literature when one considers its very "concept" as well as the discrepancy between this concept and the different histories to which it gave rise. Sadan, perhaps the greatest Israeli literary critic of the twentieth century, made clear that a historical, philosophical, and psychoanalytical understanding was essential to any reading of Hebrew literature (Sadan had also diagnosed a schizophrenic dimension in all of Jewish literature). The rigor of Sadan's distinctions and of his readings throughout his numerous studies and monographs imprinted itself on every aspect of Modern Hebrew literary practice. It has been furthered, and critically expanded, by Dan Miron. More recently, Alan Mintz has attended to the "self-conception" of Israeli literature, one carried over from pre-State Hebrew literature, and to the "status of Israeli literature as literature" in critical practice. Mintz begins his description of "the boom in Israeli fiction" with the following series of historical distinctions, a series of historical beginnings, which concisely set the stage for my own discussion here, albeit without concerning himself with, indeed, ignoring the very possibility of, Jewish literature: "Hebrew literature, which began with the Bible, has had a very, very, long history. Modern Hebrew literature, which began with the Enlightenment, has been around for two centuries. Against this time line, the Hebrew novels and short stories written in Israel since 1970 might seem callow and unproven recent arrivals."[17] One could mention many more examples where the question of methodological significance and historical specificity is addressed with more or less acknowledgment of the difficulty involved in establishing "modernity," always to argue nonetheless for and about it as the "unique problem of literary research" (as Simon Halkin puts it in his own survey of Modern Hebrew literature).[18]

In this context one may already learn from historians of nationalism who have long shown that defining the new (the moment of birth, *nasci*, of the Nation) has been a cultural task, which, in historical terms, often takes the form of a paradox. The demand for the new requires a sharp distancing from the past, an interruption made in the name of a past said to have always already been there and that must be revisited, appropriated by the new as *its* past. Put another way, the call for (cultural, literary, political) autonomy and independence may seek to establish that which was never there (a national literature, a nation-state) but must nevertheless be shown to have already been operative. This paradox may or may not make it necessary to emphasize one over the other (there is nothing new, it is really the old and has always been so, as a certain— and, ironically, quite modern—"fundamentalism" would claim; or: the new is a break from the old, which it either cancels or preserves, even resolves and heals, as the logic of the modernizing has it). Be that as it may, historians of nationalism have also pointed out that this general, indeed universal if also differential, pattern is itself modern and that its self-presentation is always accompanied by a claim for singularity.[19] In other words, nationalism is an assertion of singularity in the name and under the form of a universal ideal (as the Hebrew version has it, Jewish nationalism would make the Jews into "a nation like all the other nations, *goy ke-khol ha-goyim*"). Within these parameters, to engage in an attempt to determine the singularity of the Hebrew literary tradition is not without difficulties.

Yet it is well known that one singularity of Hebrew literature is that it must be distinguished from nationalism, from Zionism, if only because, historically, it precedes, exceeds, at times contradicts and even opposes any national project aiming for the so-called normalization of Jewish existence, that is, aiming for its participation in a national project. By now, the Zionist claim that Hebrew literature could only be written when territorial, political, and linguistic conditions would make it possible has been proven spectacularly wrong in Europe, not in Palestine, in the nineteenth and even twentieth centuries.[20] The singularity of Modern Hebrew literature lies, therefore, in another kind of distinction than a nationalist one. What is it, then, that makes Modern Hebrew literature a new, and distinct, phenomenon? What is it that it distinguishes itself from? And what are the kinds of distinctions operative in the definition of its singularity?

Modern Hebrew literature is new, which is to say that it is modern. This tautology should not obscure the variety of answers that have been offered to determine its novelty, its singularity. Without doing too much violence to this diversity, these many answers can be gathered under two general propositions:

1. Modern Hebrew literature fundamentally *breaks* with the past. It is an entirely new phenomenon that has no precedent. This radical break can be affirmed or lamented, and it can be descriptive ("there has been a break") or prescriptive ("there should be a break") or both. In other words, Modern Hebrew literature is—or should be—the *result of a crisis*.

2. Modern Hebrew literature is new but does not break with its past. It may learn from it or ignore it; it may resolve it, synthesize it, or fail to do so. Burdened with internal tensions, it remains since its beginnings, *in a state of crisis*. And here too, description and prescription coexist: crisis has either been resolved (for example, with the creation of the State of Israel), *or* it will be resolved in the future, *or* it will never be and should never be resolved.

Every historical account of Modern Hebrew literature partakes of one (or both) of these answers or set of answers to the question of its modernity and its singularity. It is also the case that each answer appeals to a different concept of history (history as a history of breaks versus history as a history of change). Yet the distinction between the two answers also reveals another, quite different, determination of the crisis, which may be illustrated in another area of literary practice, namely, in the institutional setting of its study: the university. Here one finds a certain discrepancy between the critical practice of *writing* literary history and that of *teaching* it.[21] Whatever the critical consensus—and there is none—regarding the nature of the crisis (rupture or change), it is clear that the university has articulated its own answer to the question of Hebrew literature: there is not a single program or department of Hebrew literature that refrains or would consider refraining from teaching courses covering the entirety of the history of Hebrew literature, from its ancient beginnings in the Hebrew Bible to the latest and most contemporary poem or novel of Israeli writing.[22] This is not only acknowledging and abiding by a pedagogical necessity. Nor does it impose a decision as to whether the crisis is past and resolved or continuing. Rather, the teaching of (the history of) Hebrew literature constitutes and sediments the space of Hebrew literature. It opens the space of questioning within which literary historians struggle with the question of the singularity of Hebrew literature and, most pointedly, of Modern Hebrew literature (hence, the discrepancy, as literary historians have dominantly produced a history of Modern Hebrew literature).[23] Critics, as well as writers and readers, are thus able to explore both "tradition and crisis, *masoret u-mashber*" in a historically responsible way.

Yet this institutional history reveals that the distance between the two answers (crisis as rupture, crisis as change) is something other than a disagreement about history. It may moreover reveal that, philosophically speaking, the disagreement is not as stark as it seems. This is so because both answers are *historical*, that is to say that they agree that the distinctiveness of Hebrew literature and of Modern Hebrew literature must be accounted for *historically*. Moreover, any account of historical crisis as radical rupture presupposes—much like the notion of crisis as change—a historical *continuum* under which it is ultimately subsumed. Such disappearance of the singular into a generality in the movement of history may be explained by way of Hegel's discussion of the "here, now, I," in which the very indexing of singularity is always already lost to abstraction and generality.[24] In other words, pointing to the moment of singularity (crisis as radical break) already transports that moment into a general movement of time and abstraction, into a general and continuous history. This may be a linguistic or historiographical failure, or it may be an ontological necessity, but whatever the case, it enables the coexistence of narratives of ruptures together with narratives of continuity. Indeed, one implicates the other, one is dependent on the other. Like Jewish history—and after Gershom Scholem, it is already banal to make this claim—the space of Hebrew literature is therefore fully determined by *both* "tradition" *and* "crisis," both by interruption and by continuity. A distinct understanding of history, of crisis as change or as rupture, may therefore not constitute the essential difference, the privileged criteria according to which one could separate between the two answers.

What, then, is the determining factor or element? What is the element that the two answers would not share and that would therefore fundamentally distinguish between them?

One could summarize it as follows: whereas the first answer (crisis as rupture) considers descriptively or prescriptively that the Hebrew (and later the Israeli) is no longer a Jew, the second answer (crisis as change) still insists that the Hebrew (and the Israeli) is a Jew, if a "new Jew," and even if a profoundly different Jew.[25] More precisely put, in the first case Hebrew literature is not (is no longer or should no longer be) Jewish literature. In the second case Hebrew literature is one among many Jewish literatures, if a different one (and whether or not it should continue to be so remains an altogether different question).

Let us recall that Hebrew is only one of the languages read, written, or spoken, often only memorized by Jews who, for most of their history, used other languages both privately and publicly (parts of the Bible are written in Aramaic, and so are the entire Talmud and the Zohar, both major sources of literary inspirations for the "moderns"). Some of these languages are called "Jewish languages" (Yiddish or Ladino, Judeo-Persian or Judeo-Arabic), but they may also be whatever languages were spoken and/or written in whatever specific time and place (Jews have spoken or written in Italian and in Arabic, in Russian and in German, in Spanish and in Latin, to take only a few examples). With the advent of Zionism the distinction between Hebrew and Jewish (a cultural and linguistic, as well as a political distinction), and, even more recently, the distinction between Israeli and Jewish (which further engages cultural and linguistic criteria, as well as political, religious, and even ethnic ones), continues to be the site of tensions, from within and from without. The terms may be related, even difficult to distinguish, but they are never identical. As we will see, it is the institutional field of Jewish studies (and its lack of reflection on Jewish literatures, its embrace of "Israel studies") that appears to dim and even erase this lack of identity and ensuing tensions.

By now, the distinction between the two answers we have considered may have become clear. If Modern Hebrew literature is the *result of a crisis*, which radically separates between Hebrew and Jewish, one cannot (or should not) study it as part of a continuum constituted by (premodern) Hebrew literature, since the latter is itself a part (if only in the past) of Jewish literature. Depending on whether the diagnosis is descriptive or prescriptive one would teach only Jewish literature (which includes precrisis, premodern Hebrew literature) or only Hebrew (that is, Modern) literature, or, at any rate, teach them apart from each other. If, on the other hand, Modern Hebrew literature is *in a state of crisis*, if it is the literature of the "new Jew" who still seeks his or her Jewishness, ancient or modern, then it does inscribe itself in a continuum, and it is indeed one within which it should be studied. Such a continuum would have to include both Hebrew and Jewish literature (which, unified by tradition, had been coextensive, if never identical, *before* the crisis instituted by modernity). An institutionalization of the two historical answers would demand the founding of two different kinds of departments, programs, or fields of study: one in which Jewish literature and Hebrew literature are two distinct fields; and one in which they are one and the same field. In both cases periodization and the question of history would remain essential.

Between Languages

It is at this juncture that the reality of the field reveals itself to be strikingly different from the range of scholarly positions that have been articulated about its object. Indeed, none of the curricular choices implied by these positions has been pursued, and Hebrew literature as a field of study remains fundamentally distinct from and overwhelmingly *exclusive of* Jewish literature. Jewish literature remains, with very few exceptions, without institutional backing and, for the most part, untaught.[26] To the best of my knowledge, there are only two departments of Jewish literature (or Jewish literatures) in the world, namely, at the Jewish Theological Seminary in New York and at Bar-Ilan University, Israel. But these are exceptions that strikingly confirm the rule: *there is no such field as "Jewish literatures."*[27]

This is a strange situation, especially if compared with the field of Jewish history, which both in Israel and elsewhere has long enjoyed extensive recognition.[28] It is strange if only because there would appear to be nothing inherently less manageable about the diversity of Jewish literary texts than there is about other Jewish historical materials. Hence, Dan Miron's claim that "there is no such thing as a unified Jewish literature," that there are instead "many variants of possible Jewish cultures or sub-cultures . . . two or three or four independent Jewish literatures as well as many Jewish-oriented literary developments, which evolved within the contexts of non-Jewish literatures," hardly seems to warrant a different institutionalization for Jewish literature (and much less an absence thereof) than for Jewish history, or indeed, Jewish culture.[29] Alternatively, the argument would seem to warrant *abstaining* from studying fragmented cultures, the elements of which are "independent" or evolving in widely different contexts, Jewish and non-Jewish. This is not a very plausible or likely development and not one that Miron would want to advocate. The peculiar predicament of Jewish literature as (not) an institution is itself the result of a complex history, no doubt, but it is also the consequence of a particular, even hegemonic, historical thinking, which has extended its reach, as we saw, even to literary studies, Hebrew or other. For understandable reasons periodization, contextualization, and historicization are by now recurring *mots d'ordre* in the humanities. Abiding by them, the field of Hebrew literature has structured itself as historical, opening the space of Hebrew literature as "tradition and crisis." Yet it is this very same historical thinking that has also refigured the complex relations existing between Hebrew literature and Jewish literature as *chronological*, as historical relations that are thought of as either inclusive or exclusive. Inclusive in that Jewish literatures are seen as trends to be included in the development of Hebrew literature or, alternatively, as part of a general phenomenon that includes both Hebrew and Jewish literatures (solutions advocated respectively by Dov Sadan and Ruth Wisse, either of which has yet to gain any institutional ground, any institutional implementation in any department or program of Jewish studies or Hebrew literature—with the exception, perhaps, of Yiddish literature—but this last "field" conjures very different issues).

Alternatively, one witnesses a more exclusive institutional relation between Hebrew and Jewish literatures such that there is (or should be) an unbridgeable difference, a difference in kind between Hebrew and Jewish literatures (Baruch Kurzweil and Yonathan Ratosh being the two extremes that meet, as Dan Miron has shown, who lament or advocate that separation). Yet, as we saw, the two institutions that have existing departments of Jewish literature never went so far as to create *another* department for the study of "non-Jewish [i.e., no longer Jewish] Hebrew literature."

Such dialectics of (theoretical, if not practical) inclusion/exclusion are representative of literary studies as a whole. Indeed, the expansion of the boundaries of the literary object, spearheaded by the critique of its aesthetic autonomy—an autonomy that itself has a long and conflicted history—has reached new heights not only with the increased significance of historical thinking already mentioned (the New Historicism and Cultural Studies are general and, perhaps, recognizable headers here) but also with the opening or widening of psychological, social, political, and cultural entryways into the realm of the literary. Under the general heading of the significance of literature, the literary object has had to include (or has been shown to exclude) "other" realms of material and intellectual life. In Jewish and Hebrew literature the significance of feminism and gender criticism has no doubt provided the most convincing illustration of this trend (from Esther Fuchs's discussion of the participation or nonparticipation of women in the prose writing scene to Dan Miron's account of early women poets, Lily Ratok's anthology of women's short stories, and Yael Feldman's recent synthesis on the work of Hebrew female novelists).[30] But there are others (I am thinking here of the work of Ross Brann and Yosef Tobi on cultural dynamics in medieval Arab Jewish writings, of Dan Miron's early and subtle renderings of the sociohistorical context of Hebrew and Israeli poetry and prose, of Ammiel Alcalay's radical refiguring of Hebrew literature along a Mediterranean cultural and geographical axis, of Arthur Lesley's call for a reconsideration of rhetorical criticism in Medieval Hebrew literature, of Chana Kronfeld's rethinking of the category "modernism" out of a renewed consideration of Hebrew and Yiddish writers, or of Hannan Hever's work, as undoing the Modern Hebrew canon and as rearticulating another inclusive/exclusive relationship, that of religion and literature in Modern Hebrew poetry. I am thinking finally, of Amnon Raz-Krakotzkin's account of the invention of "Jewish literature" by Christian censorship in the sixteenth century and of Yitzhak Laor's vitriolic critique of Israeli literature as collaborating with the worst).

Finally, perhaps, what is revealed by a consideration of the dialectics of inclusion and exclusion operating within the question of Hebrew literature, between Hebrew literature and Jewish literature, is a peculiar failure of historical thinking. For none of the distinct historical arguments we have considered have enabled or succeeded in enabling a strict separation between Hebrew and Jewish literatures. Indeed, except for Ratosh and the "Young Hebrews" or "Canaanites" no one ever realistically considered implementing such a separation, the very absolute separation that nonetheless *remains the institutional reality in Hebrew literature departments and programs* where the historical study of Hebrew literature remains fundamentally cut off from the systematic study of Jewish literatures. If anything, the *historical* arguments we have followed demonstrate that the two terms are indeed distinct, not at all coextensive, if fundamentally indissociable as their relationship structures, throughout history, any historical understanding of Hebrew literature. In other words, throughout history, Hebrew and Jewish literatures have remained heterogeneous and indissociable. What is clear is that they could not be located diachronically (Hebrew then Jewish, Jewish then Hebrew, depending on where one begins), nor could the difference between them be defined as particularly "modern" (not, at least, if one uses the term historically).

Without contesting, therefore, the relative autonomy of *Modern* Hebrew literature, or calling for an increased institutionalization of Jewish literature, what remains is the question of the space of Hebrew literature as a field of study.[31] It is a field that continues to be structured by a "schizoid" history (as Sadan diagnosed it) in which no strict or even desirable autonomy has ever been established, either of the Hebrew vis-à-vis the Jewish, or of the Jewish vis-à-vis the non-Jewish, or of the literary vis-à-vis the nonliterary.[32] What appears (or disappears) in modern discourse as the distinct relation (and nonrelation, even rupture) of Jewish and Hebrew literature (figured as exteriorities that *no longer* constitute a whole) becomes, within the space of Hebrew literature as a fully established disciplinary field, an urgent, perhaps insurmountable, *historical* difficulty: It is because historical thinking governs the field, and because Hebrew literature is said to have a longevity and a continuity that puts it on a par with Sanskrit and Chinese (as Robert Alter suggests), that it has to contend with the undoing, the fragmentation of its very history, the undoing of the "Hebrew-ness" of this history, an undoing that makes it impossible to write (or teach) a history of Hebrew literature without relating to and reading texts in Aramaic, Greek, Arabic, Spanish, Italian, Yiddish, French, and other languages (hence Alter can waver between the "polyglot nature of Hebrew *texts*," as well as the "polyglot *context* of Hebrew literature," implicitly affirming the principled, if not actual, "victory" of Dov Sadan's call for expansion and synthesis of Hebrew and Jewish literatures). This very impossibility, rather than any empirically based literary history, is what has been institutionalized in a study of Hebrew literature "as such." But the history of Hebrew literature is not, nor can it ever be, the history of *Hebrew* literature. As a *history* that governs understanding and never quite breaks with the past—i.e., the (Aramaic) Talmud, (Arabic and Judeo-Arabic) Maimonides, (Judeo-Arabic) Yehuda ha-Levi, and the (Aramaic) Zohar all the way to Persian and Judeo-Persian, Italian, Arabic, French, and, of course, Yiddish and English—Hebrew literature as a literature in the Hebrew language cannot but fail to include this very past which is not one: neither past, nor a unified one. Nor can it resolve this historical problem simply by growing more inclusive. Indeed, it is the duty of historical thinking to consider the singularity of each period and therefore the dynamics of inclusion and exclusion that institute themselves vis-à-vis distinct "others" and according to different historical limits. And it is this very problem that could constitute the nature of the singularity of Hebrew literature, a singularity that exceeds, therefore, all periodizations as such and all attempts to contain the "schizoid" or "traditionally unified" dimension to any particular period. What one could call the empirical reality of Medieval, Renaissance, and Modern Hebrew literature as "polyglot" has always already constituted a *comparative literature.*

Paul de Man has suggested that the nature of the debate between the ancients and the moderns had "forced the participants to make *comparative* critical evaluations of ancient versus contemporary readings."[33] Doing so, de Man seems to confirm that the issue is an empirical one and that it could therefore be resolved by practices of inclusion, further institutionalization, or more efficient categorization, and so forth.[34] But against this reading de Man offers another sense of the comparative as a dimension "internal" to literature. "Literature," he writes, "exists at the same time in the modes of error and truth; it both betrays and obeys its own mode of being" (163). This internal tension, this treacherous obedience of literature constitutes "the distinctive character of literature," and it "becomes manifest as an inability to escape from a condition that is felt to be unbearable" (162). This inner tension, this "inherent conflict," cannot be institutionalized, even if it operates within the institution, as well as without. It is what de Man has described as a going to war of texts and with texts, "written texts" that "masquerade in the guise of wars or revolutions," and of wars that masquerade as texts.[35] Comparative literature, in such a context—and it is the context within which we find ourselves—goes to war in the mode of betrayal. Throughout and against history, literature resists. Literature is that which resists historicization, a linguistically and generically fragmented field rather than a unified one.[36] To name this fragmented, resisting field, to name it provisionally and locally, as it were, and to name it "Jewish literature," to do so in the context of Hebrew literary studies, in the context of Jewish studies, thus answers to a number of necessities. But the difficulties to which this naming bears witness must further be thought of as the *disappearance* of the space of literature as common space, and its becoming comparative. It is the disappearance of the *modern* singularity of Hebrew literature and of its linguistic, national, and even historical integrity as *Hebrew* literature. If the history of Hebrew literature is not "its" history (but the history of Jewish literatures), if Hebrew literature is not *Hebrew* literature (because Hebrew is not its language, as Laor compellingly demonstrates), if the institution of Hebrew literature is the forceful inscription of its failure as institution, and if, finally, the space of Hebrew literature is not to be found in Hebrew literature nor in Hebrew literary modernity, then Hebrew literature disappears.[37] To acknowledge this disappearance—no longer a hypothetical one—within Hebrew literary studies is, for the critic, primarily "an act of critical judgment directed against himself." De Man singularly affirms this role of the literary critic, who produces acknowledgments of such disappearances, as the role of a traitor, one of a peculiar kind. He has to perform his task "with full knowledge that he thus destroys his own project, with the hatred of the traitor for the camp that he has chosen to join" (161). And his treason, which is also an active joining (a treacherous obedience), a belonging without allegiance, perhaps, is the promise, no more than a promise and, equally, the threat of another future, if not of another modernity. "Then," writes Friedrich Nietzsche, quoted by de Man, "then it will become clear how illegitimate the existence of something, of a privilege, a caste or a dynasty actually is, and how much it deserves to be destroyed. Then the past is judged, critically attacked at its very roots with a sharp knife, and brutally cut down, regardless of established pieties. This is always a dangerous process, dangerous for life itself."[38]

4

'Eber va-'Arab (The Arab Literature of the Jews)

> When one literature contains details which have their legitimate place in the other, an interdependence may be assumed.
> —S. D. Goitein, *Jews and Arabs*

> Thus, paradoxically, the "people of the book" learned to write books from the very culture that bestowed the name upon them.
> —R. P. Scheindlin, "Merchants and Intellectuals"

I

In the beginning, there was no beginning.[1] There was and there was not—at once and in order of succession, repetition, or filiation. In the beginning there was life; that is to say, there was narrative and genealogy, genealogy as narrative. For "narrative begins with the story or history of humankind [*l'histoire de l'humanité*]. . . . [N]arrative is simply there like life itself [*comme la vie*]."[2] In the beginning there was comparative literature, the comparison of life with literature, literature lifelike. There was a father too, no more than one, perhaps, more than one, which is to say, more than one name. For the name of the father that is not one is simultaneously and successively Abram or Abraham or Ibrahim. At the beginning there was abandonment and repetition. Of the name and of the fathers. And all this happens, so the story goes, before we even get to the sons, who are the real, fictional, and repetitive beginning after the beginning, and of which there were at least two, but only one that counts, once one counts and recounts, gives an account or a narrative, for them. The one that counts is the one, but he could be anything or anyone, divine, human, or animal. Repeatable, substitutable (the one for the oth-

ers, one brother for the other, any other for the one god), he is, from
the beginnings, part of a sacrificial economy, a circle of exchange and of
substitution.[3] He is the one that was and was not abandoned, that was
and was not sacrificed. But before him, before them, before the father
and the son, before the fathers, the sons and the brothers, and the others, that is to say, before the beginning, there was yet another beginning,
namely, *their* father—if he is one, and if he has a name. According to
one narrative at least, one in which he does have a name, it is the father
(here named Terah) who not only begins the whole story but also initiates the abandonment before abandonment, the leave-taking and depart-
ing motion without which no story could ever be, if a story there must
be. "Hero leaves [parents'] home," classified Vladimir Propp.[4] Granted,
Terah is the father, not the hero, but at this stage the difference may be
moot since he is the only agent. It is he who "took his son Abram [*way-
iqqah Terah et Abram beno*], his grandson Lot the son of Haran, and his
daughter-in-law the wife of Abram, and made them leave [*vayyetz'u itam*]
Ur of the Chaldeans to go [to] the land of Canaan" (Gen. 11:31).

In the beginning, the other beginning (but there are more), it is
not this father who takes his son to leave and go to Canaan. Rather, God
rehearses and repeats the desire of the father by beginning it all anew,
substituting himself for the father and commanding Abram to abandon
his father, ordering him to leave him and everything behind, to boldly
go where his father had said he wanted to lead before him. Where? There
where, it turns out, he, the father, may not have wanted to go after
all—this story, at any rate, this beginning, does not say. "Yahweh said to
Abram: 'Leave [*lekh lekha*] your country, your family and your father's
house, for the land I will show you'" (Gen. 12:1). Thus Abram becomes
the father, if there is one. And, having abandoned everything, his name,
the other one, and certainly *not the first one*, is established as that which
will be remembered. Or so it is commanded. "I will make you a great
nation; I will bless you and make your name so famous [*va-agadelah
shemekha*] that it will be used as a blessing" (Gen. 12:2). In the beginning
was the (second) name, and it is not one: at once a blessing and a curse.
"I will bless those who bless you: I will curse those who slight you. All the
tribes of the earth shall bless themselves by you" (Gen. 12:3).

Like the first name, the father, the other one, the abandoned one, will never be heard of again. Narrative begins there where abandonment inscribes the abandoned one as nonbeginning, as otherwise than beginning. If it must begin, or if it must, at least, begin somewhere, narrative begins with displacement and translation. Reading the father of monotheism, the father and monotheism, Fethi Benslama explains that the more proximate one gets to such abandoned origins, to this principle of the father—the father as principle—as the origin, the more father figures are bound to be encountered, entertained, and abandoned, as well as narrated. Benslama also underscores that the relations between these fathers and father figures cannot be expressed or conceived in a linear or fixed fashion. Rather, there is always repetition, a play of the proper and improper, a play of appropriation and de-propriation, what Benslama calls "un jeu de transpropriation du père." Benslama writes: "There is Abraham, at the top of monotheistic genealogy, a father who engenders himself by way of his ability to detach from the tyrannical and murderous figure of the Originary Father."[5]

But that was only the beginning. Of which, as can be plainly read in the story, there was not one, but a succession of repetitions. In the beginning, then, there was and there was not a father. He is there in the first place, but he is not the beginning. And so there was life (and with it, the ambiguous seeds of heterosexual, reproductive normativity as abandonment: "This is why a man leaves his father and mother ['al-ken ya'azov ish et aviv ve-et immo] and joins himself to his wife"), that is to say, narrative.[6] There was filiation, and the "potentially murderous outcome of bearing children," in a manner such that one keeps getting the persistent impression that "few things are as problematic and as universally fraught as what we might have supposed to be the mere natural continuity between one generation and the next."[7] Clearly, there were already, and from the beginning, "difficulties of filiation"; there was "the breaking of ties with family, home, class, country, and traditional beliefs as necessary stages in the achievement of spiritual and intellectual freedom."[8] There was both filiation and affiliation. There was, twice, "Abraham, Abraham!" and there were the fathers. There was war too, and there was crime and punishment; there were women, sisters, and mothers who could create and procreate, and who could repeat other stories, with different beginnings. Yet in the beginnings, so this story goes, there were fathers and forefathers, those abandoned and those found, and there was—or so it seems—the father.[9] And then there was the enemy. The enemy is the father. This is the story of Abraham as it was repeated, recited, from the beginning:

And convey unto them the story of Abraham [*naba'a Ibrahim*] [how it was] when he asked his father and his people, "What is it that you worship?" They answered: "We worship idols, and we remain ever devoted to them." Said he: "Do [you really think that] they hear you when you invoke them, or benefit you or do you harm? They exclaimed: "But we found our forefathers doing the same [*bal wajadnaa abaa'ana kadhalika yaf'alun*]. Said [Abraham]: "Have you, then, ever considered what it is that you have been worshipping, you and those ancient forefathers of yours?" "Now [as for me, I know that,] verily, these [false deities] are my enemies ['*aduwwul-lii*], [and that none is my helper] save the Sustainer of all the worlds.[10]

And that, to repeat, was just the beginning.

2

Where to begin, then, in order to recite and narrate or at least to recount, and account for, the relation between fathers, between sons, and fathers and sons, between the Hebrew ('*Eber*) and the Arab ('*Arab*), the Jew, the Arab, between Hebrew, Jewish, and Arabic narrative and literature? "If one were to write a comprehensive history of Judeo-Arabic literature, one would extend the limits at both ends, to the sixth century and to our own time, respectively."[11] Such story or history could extend further to Mount Moriah, in Jerusalem, or to the Ka'ba (which, some traditions have it, was built by Abraham and Ishmael). But should it begin with Abraham, Isaac, and Ishmael (Sarah and Hagar) or with Ka'b al-Akhbar? In the Mashreq or in the Maghreb? With religion or with literature? With disputation or with translation?[12] With the Midrash (this large and multifarious, multigenerational compendium of rabbinic lore) or with the *Isra'iliyyat* (those traditions said to find their origin in Jewish lore)? With Sa'adya b. Joseph al-Fayyumi (Sa'adya Gaon) and Samaw'al al-Maghribi or with the Kahina, Rabbi Israel Najjarah and the "hundreds of manuscripts" that were left by North African, Arab Jewish "scholars from the seventeenth to the nineteenth century," all of whom worked "in every genre, from the exegesis of the great traditional texts to collections of poetry and historical chronicles of their community"?[13] Or later yet with Ya'qub Sannu' and Shim'on Ballas, Emile Habiby or Anton Shammas?[14] With the modern invention of the Semites or with the "actual" Semites (as if they ever existed)? In poetry or in prose? In the past or in the present?

In the beginning there was comparative literature, and there were the possibilities and impossibilities of identifying an entry point, much less a beginning, that would not be a repetition of the same old story. This has little to do with the reciprocal claims and counterclaims of primacy, historical or other, made by both "sides" (as if there were such, and only two at that, as if *that* was the problem), claims that assume not only the importance of the first, explicitly undermined by all repeated beginnings, and certainly by those we have begun to consider, but also the purity of origins, embracing the widespread fiction (but what is there, here, if not fiction and narrative?) of an event in which everything that is to become was already there at the beginning. In such narrative, "Judaism" precedes "Islam" even if the Talmud (which determines the nature of what must still be called "rabbinic Judaism" and its historical descendants) would never have gained the currency it has without the spread of Islam, even if none of what is known today as "Judaism," as Jewish or as Hebrew culture, could ever have become what it is without the momentous changes affecting everything from grammar to theology, from ethics to literature, from law to philosophy, without the unification of most of the Jewish world brought about by Islam, a unification that is paralleled only by Hellenism and not even by the modern spread of Anglo culture.[15] Everything changed. And this to the point that Jews became, as it were, Arabs. Minimally, and "for all intents and purposes, then, Jews and Christians living in the Arabian Peninsula were culturally and ethnically Arab."[16] Furthermore, "it is clear that sixth- and seventh-century Judaisms were still in a state of flux as rabbinic Judaism was establishing itself as the dominant and soon to be virtual monopolistic expression of the religion of Israel. It would be a grave error to assume, *a priori*, that the kind (or kinds) of Judaism believed and practiced by seventh-century Arabian Jews [or any Jews, for that matter] was the same as that of

Maimonides in twelfth-century Egypt."[17] And, as Aziz al-Azmeh shows at length in the case of political doctrine and practice, the same goes for "Islam." Al-Azmeh calls attention to a larger, more general, problem when he documents the way in which "classical Muslim forms" are conceived of as having been "born somewhat complete, and then stumbled upon the necessity of various forms of accommodation with the ambient world; their histories are consequently often construed as nothing but decline and degeneration." What is rather necessary, al-Azmeh counters, is to show that "the genesis of a diverse body of specifically Muslim forms of the enunciation of power required a number of centuries, that these forms were by no means *sui generis*, and that Muslim enunciations of power, even affirmations of its sacrality, were not necessarily the work of a specifically religious discourse."[18] We will return to some more marginal questions regarding the role and function of "religion" in the story we are reading, but for now suffice it to underscore that the phrase "enunciations of power" is one of the names of "narrative."[19]

An alternative point of departure, another beginning, has to engage the difficulties posed by the very limits drawn by the question of relation or of comparison. Indeed, any understanding of the relation between Arabic and Hebrew will have to take into account that the matter far exceeds the apparent linguistic dimension to which we should have to confine ourselves. To illustrate this, one example will suffice, from an anthology of "imaginative narratives from classical Hebrew literature" in which the only room allocated to Arabic "influence" is reserved to the *maqama*.[20] One can account for this particular phenomenon by way of the significance of poetry rather than prose or narrative as the privileged realm of literary exchanges between Hebrew and Arabic. Aside from the inaccurate view thus produced (since it ignores countless narrative sites to which we will return), we will see that issues of genre are certainly essential to address. For now, however, it is important to stress that the problem of literary relations is a much larger one than either language or genre. For how are we to construe the "sides" involved in our descriptions? Once again, to speak of Arabic and Hebrew in the restricted, linguistic sense will not do since numerous sites of the "relation" all belong, strictly speaking, to one language and one language only: Arabic (later, to Hebrew mainly, although never to Hebrew only). Alternatively, it would be impossible to measure the significance of said relation without taking into account other languages, whether Aramaic, Persian, and Turkish, but also Italian, French, and Spanish, and even English (and no doubt others), where echoes of the phenomena we are trying to describe continue to be felt while awaiting a full scholarly account. One minimal corrective, then, would be to consider the extensive material under consideration in an inclusive manner, namely, as having to do with *Arab Jewish letters*. Addressing one of the early examples of Arab Jewish narrative, in fact "one of the most popular Jewish-Arabic compilations"[21]—Nissim b. Jacob Ibn Shahin's *Kitab al-Faraj ba'd ash-Shiddah*—William Brinner provides a succinct account of the reasons underlying the necessity for such corrective:

During the eleventh and twelfth centuries of the Christian era, after some four hundred years of close contact with Muslim civilization, a new Jewish cultural flowering took place, using two vehicles of expression: the Hebrew language, kept alive as a literary tongue and undergoing a steady enrichment and expansion to fill new needs, and Judeo-Arabic, the common language of the masses of Jews living in the Arabic-speaking world from Iraq in the East to the Atlantic coast of Morocco and Spain in the West. . . . A new stream of literary borrowings, mainly from Muslim literature, entered Jewish literature via Judeo-Arabic, either in the form of themes and genres or—by way of translation—whole works.[22]

3

Let us begin again, in medias res, with a story or a legend, at any rate, a narrative reported by a modern scholar, and let us recall the words of Shlomo Goitein, who asserted, in a relevant context, that "there are, of course, many legends, both Jewish and Arab, about the origins of the Jewish community in Arabia. Nor is there any lack of scientific conjecture—the modern form of legend—on the subject."[23] The scholar, then, tells us a story. According to this story, there is a "tradition about a group of Jews who embraced Islam, but asked the Prophet's permission to observe the Sabbath and to study the Torah at night. They were, of course, denied this permission. A verse of the Qur'an (Sura 2:208) was revealed about it. According to Ibn Kathir (Tafsir 1:329) Muhammad said: 'Believe in the Torah, the Zabur and the Evangel, but the Qur'an should suffice you.'"[24] This is only one of numerous traditions, one among many "stories or legends that are specifically designated by medieval Muslim scholars as Israelite Tales," most of which "cannot be found in Jewish literature—at least not as they are found in Islamic sources."[25] Many of these tales were put aside or excluded over the course of the centuries, but they continue to be a living source of debate and dispute, all of which involve the inclusion or dismissal of famous individuals, fathers and forefathers, and chains of transmissions, filiation and affiliation. These are narratives and embedded narratives, including the many that "appear to have all the basic qualities of the Israelite Tales without having been excluded from the major works." Indeed, "only those traditions that have been considered inappropriate to Islamic doctrine are branded as Israelite Tales."[26] As far as tales and narratives go, then, they may all be said at one point or another to amount to nothing, as narratives often are. Rashid Rida, for example, was engaged in such a critique of Israelite Tales at the beginning of the twentieth century, claiming that "these accounts are nothing but *Isra'iliyyat* which have neither a sound transmission nor anything reliable in them."[27] Rida's disciple, Mahmoud Abu Rayya, pursued that line of thought by establishing an alternative, and secure, chain of tradition, the beginnings of which could be found in Ka'b al-Akhbar, who would have been, Abu Rayya says, "the first Zionist."[28] Narrative and genealogy, filiation and affiliation underscore the layering, indeed, the palimpsest, that gives reason to the other's narrative and testifies, within traditions as broken and unbroken chains, continuous and discontinuous genealogies, to the lingering effects of Arab Jewish letters. "Believe in the Torah, the Zabur and the Evangel, but the Qur'an should suffice you."

4

The story on narratives in Arab Jewish letters hardly appears to be a major, let alone a classical one. For all intents and purposes, and until modern times at least, the main plot, the action, takes place elsewhere. Poetry is often the means that counts, and philosophy too, which, incidentally, does involve allegory and, therefore, narrative.[29] But that is—again—only the beginning. We have seen that, with Sa'adya Gaon, everything begins anew and radically changes within "Judaism," a beginning and a change that figures and refigures the relation between Hebrew and Arab narrative—who's on first?—indeed, within Hebrew and Arab Jewish letters in general. The narrative is changed, and the order of appearance is reversed. As one critic puts it, "Hebrew grammar, lexicography, poetic composition, epistolography, and narrative all were fundamentally changed by the example and influence of Arabic activity in these fields."[30] But what is narrative? As the epic poem or the *maqama* demonstrate, narrative can take many forms, not all of which are simply prose, although such is dominantly the case. The difficulty of determining what narrative is and where to look for it in Hebrew and Jewish literature, however, may have less to do with the dispute between poetry and prose (a recurring dispute) than with the fact that "medieval Hebrew rhetoric has scarcely been studied until now."[31] Whether in the study, translation, and commentary of classical rhetoric or in the dominant interest in poetry ("Because Arabic poetry was considered to be the highest kind of literary expression, distinguished by meter and extended rhyme, it is the treatises about poetry that present the norms that also apply to unmetrical expression, prose"),[32] whether in philosophical allegoresis or in the profound engagement in the pursuit of *'adab* ("Jewish writers in the Muslim setting adopted and partly judaized *'adab*. To translate the term, in both its reference to the range of cultivated skills and to the propaedeutics of philosophy, Hebrew used *musar*. This term suggests the didactic and moralistic justification implied for the studies included under it, as well as a wide range of genres that one of its components, rhetoric, could govern"),[33] it is clear that the question of narrative exceeds the recognizable issues of filiation and affiliation, that it demands that one consider and reconsider what Peggy Kamuf has called "the division of literature," within a broad understanding of literature as the general field of writing.[34] The rhetorical and philosophical treatises of Maimonides or of Moses Ibn 'Ezra,[35] the *musar* literature of Bahya Ibn Paquda (in *Kitab al-hidaya 'ila fara'id al-qulub*, translated into Hebrew as *hovot Ha-levavot*), and after him and the *tafsir* or biblical commentaries of Sa'adya Gaon or Abraham Ibn 'Ezra, the numerous *maqamat* extant in both Hebrew and Arabic by Jewish writers, as well as other narrative texts or collections among which are Ibn Shahin's *Kitab al-Faraj*, Yosef Ibn Zabara's *Sefer Sha'ashu'im*, Solomon Ibn Saqbel's "Asher in the Harem,"[36] Judah Ibn Shabbetai's "The Misogynist," Yehuda ha-Levi *Kitab ar-radd wad-dalil fid-din adh-dhalil* (better known as the *Kuzari*), Isaac Ibn Sahula's *Mashal ha-Kadmoni* (and there are others), and the book, even inspired "novel," written or disseminated by Ibn Sahula's own neighbor in Guadalajara,[37] perhaps even his friend and associate, Moses of Leon—namely, one of the single most impressive, and successful, literary achievements in the whole of Jewish literature, and the most important work of Kabbalah, the Zohar—all these raise a plethora of questions as to where to look for narrative in Arab Jewish letters. As Arthur Lesley puts it, "[A]ll this is unexplored territory, because the questions have not previously been asked."[38] Furthermore, "questions about the continuity of modern Hebrew literature with medieval Hebrew will become tractable, and interesting again, only when the contours of medieval Hebrew literature, poetry, and prose, have been drawn more systematically."[39]

The obstacles remain numerous, and the Zohar provides a pertinent and revealing example. Consider that it emerges in thirteenth-century Castille and that it is with its appearance that "the allegorical use of narrative reaches its full maturity. . . . Almost Joycean in its imaginative and linguistic ingenuity," the Zohar is, moreover, written at once as the revival of ancient, midrashic Aramaic and as the invention of *vernacular* literature, which was occurring all over the Western Mediterranean at the time.[40] Yet when the Zohar addresses the issue of narrative in a thematically explicit way, difficulties begin: "Woe to that man who asserts that the Torah came to show us mere stories and profane matters. For if this were so, we too could compose a Torah today, one that would deal with profane matters, a Torah worthy of even greater praise!"[41] As David Stern explains, by "mere stories and profane matters," what the Zohar refers to is "the narratives in the Bible, the stories of the patriarchs and their descendants, the children of Israel." What the Zohar intends, in other words, is to consider narrative as genealogy and genealogy as narrative, filiation and affiliation. What the Zohar performs, however, is a certain division, a rupture and a departure in which imitation and outdoing are ostensibly declared as being within reach of its literary genius. Far from constituting "the sheer disparagement of narrative writing" (and how could it when its entire endeavor is framed and structured, constituted and traversed by narrative?) or a "disdain for fictional narrative," the author of the Zohar at once boasts that he has the genial capacity to outdo the Torah—and that he may very well have achieved the creation of a "Torah worthy of even greater praise"—and does so by interrupting, dividing and restarting, indeed recreating, the literary tradition within which he also inscribes himself.[42] Beginning again—and the Zohar's elaborations of layers of narrative and narrated commentaries are constituted by a luxurious proliferation of beginnings—the Zohar is indeed "a kabbalistic re-creation of midrash."[43] As Ammiel Alcalay aptly describes it, the Zohar is "that most unclassifiable of books, itself an amalgam of the narrative, poetic, and mystical conglomerate cutting through Christian Spain" and the Muslim world. Subsequently, it "infiltrated almost every aspect of the spiritual, communal, and intellectual life of the Jewish Levant."[44] Written in Aramaic, the Zohar remains one of the classical highlights of medieval narrative prose, an event in the history of Hebrew literature and of Arab Jewish letters. Indeed, were the Zohar and kabbalah as a whole (much of which was written, expanded, commented upon, and refashioned in the Arab-speaking world, whether in Fez and Tripoli, or Safed and Baghdad, and the nature of which is, to a great extent, literary, whether prose or verse, poetic or narrative) to be included in the history of literature, it would inevitably be seen as having long demanded a new division of literature, a reconsideration of that which separates poetry and prose, mysticism and literature, Hebrew and Arabic.

5

No discussion of narrative can escape the question of language. This question, which may be formulated otherwise as the question of craft or of inspiration, locates the articulation of a link to conditions of production, to material sources or authorities in which the narrative finds its origins or out of which it grows. Such articulation may be left implicit, or it may be described at length, but it is an essential moment that concerns the coming to be of narrative, that is to say, the "ground" for a narrative or scholarly account of narrative's becoming narrative. Not unlike the relation between ground and figure, which can hardly be maintained in most cases, the place or ground of which Arab Jewish writers speak is often vanishing. The most famous and striking narrative of such vanishing, which also provides the occasion for an elaborate and polemical reflection on the relations between Hebrew and Arabic, appears in the extended narrative with which Yehuda al-Harizi opens his *Tahkemoni*—a collection of Hebrew *maqamat* that found its original, later vanishing, inspiration in the work of his illustrious predecessor, al-Hariri, whom he had earlier translated:

Now the thing that stirred up my spirit to compose this book was that a wise man among the sages of the Arabs [*me-hakhmey yishme'elim*] and one of the choicest of the enlightened whose tongue is powerful in Arabic poetry [*bi-melizot 'arab*] and through whose mouth the vision of song is spread abroad—he is the famous al-Hariri, all the authors of poetry except him are barren—he composed a book in the Arabic tongue that offers goodly words. Although its themes are hewn from the Hebrew tongue and all its excellent metaphors are taken and handed over from our books.[45]

Castigating those who took the Hebrew tongue and "cast her into the pit," those who "spurned the Hebrew tongue and made love to the tongue of Hagar [*ve-kullam ma'asu leshon 'ibriya ve-hashqu leshon hagariya*]," having seen that "Hagar had borne lovely sons while Sarai a barren life led,"[46] the author decides to "compose this book to show the strength of the Holy tongue to the holy people whose eyes are bedaubed that they cannot see, their thoughts that they cannot understand." He takes pains to emphasize that "in all the things that I have mentioned in this book—not a thing have I taken from the book of the Arab (al-Hariri) except it be through forgetfulness or by chance and I knew it not. But all the themes of this book were created out of my own mind, new, recently come up, issued forth from the fountain of Judah."[47]

In an example that recalls this conclusion, the author of what is considered the first Hebrew *maqama*, Solomon Ibn Saqbel, had commented on the nature of his narrative construction by enjoining his readers not to be taken in by what they heard since what he wrote is "a tale of lover's folly this, no more, a pack of lies / I made up every word [*ha-lo hen*

la 'agey 'ogvim u-milim / asher bada yedidekhem milevavo]."[48] More directly
relevant to the matter of language, Yehuda ha-Levi does tell a tale (the
report of the conversion of the king of the Khazars and the subsequent,
fictional and philosophical, dialogue between the king and a rabbi) and
even explains that, as a result of having "found among the arguments of
the Rabbi, many which appealed to me and were in harmony with my
own opinions, I resolved to write them down exactly as they had been
spoken."[49] Ha-Levi proceeds to "wink at his audience, acknowledging
an element of fiction in both the frame story and his own remark, not-
ing that 'the wise will understand.'"[50] But ha-Levi strangely leaves out
the question of his own language choice, remaining silent on the issue.
Aside from being one of the most brilliant among the medieval Hebrew
poets, ha-Levi is "a scholar equally conversant in philosophy, law, poetry,
theology and mysticism, one whose talents and sensibility enable him to
perceive common threads and forge innovative connections," a singular individual who "presents classical Judaism using the new experiential
language emerging in medieval Islam" and doing all of this in Arabic.[51]
In fact, ha-Levi "uses and transforms Arabic terminology to present his
unique view of Jewish religious experience," as well as his views on language, literature, and history. And "because he is writing in Arabic, Ha-
Levi is forced to use certain Islamic religious terms. As a Judeo-Arabic
writer, however, he also has the choice to introduce Hebrew terms and
phrases. It is thus fruitful to ask why he chooses the Arabic terms he
does, to investigate the Islamic context of these terms, and to analyze the
way he builds upon or subverts their contextual meaning."[52] It should
also be fruitful to ask why he chooses—rather than being forced (and by
what or by whom?)—to write in Arabic rather than in Hebrew. Clearly,
ha-Levi follows a logic not unlifelike (Arabic was after all lingua franca).
He follows a well-established convention, one instituted by "the founder
of Judeo-Arabic literature," Sa'adya Gaon, and one that distributed different purposes and functions between the two languages: "Hebrew as
the ceremonial language and Arabic as the language for communication
of specific information."[53] One should nonetheless recall that just a few
decades later, the great Maimonides himself decided to write a book that
also belongs to the new patterns established by Arab Jewish letters, and
in doing so he too was initiating a new beginning, attempting "to start

the history of rabbinic law all over again with a new canonical work."
Maimonides wrote this book, the *Mishneh Torah*, "after decades of writing nearly exclusively in Arabic." Yet he chose to write this one in Hebrew. "Possibly his choice of language was dictated by his growing awareness of the Jewish readership outside the Islamic sphere."[54] Possibly. In his own choice, at any rate, ha-Levi appears to break with at least one predecessor, himself a great beginning, namely, and again, Sa'adya. For no one before him "had ever made an issue of the study of the language itself, demanding that, for the sake of Torah, Jews master Hebrew, study its grammar, and even learn to speak in it. No one before him had attempted to explain the status of the Hebrew language in terms of world history."[55] Break or continuity—filiation or affiliation—what matters is no doubt that ha-Levi's choice is inscribed within the history of Arab Jewish letters, a choice that implicates at once—simultaneously and sequentially—Hebrew and Arabic, and Aramaic as well. Ha-Levi himself provides a narrative and philological account of the relation among these languages, offering the rudiments of a possible commentary regarding his writing the book in Arabic, a book, moreover, within which are praised the hyperbolically superior qualities of the Hebrew tongue—from the beginning, that is, before Abraham—its singular rapport to other languages and the distinction between Holy Tongue and vernacular at the outer edge, as it were, of Arabic:

Considered historically and logically, its original form is the noblest [*wa-hiya fi dhatiha ashraf naqlan wa-qiyasan*]. According to tradition, it is the language in which God spoke to Adam and Eve, and in which the latter conversed. . . . The whole is traced back to 'Eber, Noah and Adam. It is the language of 'Eber after whom it is called Hebrew, because after the confusion of tongues it was he who retained it. Abraham was an Aramean of Ur Kasdim, because the language of the Chaldeans was Aramaic. He employed Hebrew as a special holy language and Aramaic for everyday use. For this reason, Ishmael brought it to the Arabic speaking nations, and the consequence was that Aramaic, Arabic and Hebrew are similar to each in their vocabulary, grammatical rules, and formation. The superiority of Hebrew is manifest from the logical point of view.[56]

As we have seen, the Zohar too builds on the distinction between languages—here between Hebrew and Aramaic—asserting the sacred superiority of the former, while using the latter as a privileged vernacular that is also the sole property of human beings (as opposed to one available to angelic beings). The Zohar's relation to Aramaic at once initiates and marks a historico-theological turning point, a narrative beginning at which dissemination and publicization, indeed the revelation, popularization, and vulgarization—the becoming-vernacular—of kabbalah as exegetical, liturgical, and narrative practice all become possible. Incidentally, one of the most famous stories about the Zohar's dissemination involves Arab intermediaries, enabling agents carrying it forward.[57] Unless situated within Arab Jewish letters, then, and the history of vernacular literatures, this turning point, indeed, this beginning, remains unthinkable. And to think it, what better guide than Maimonides, who figures and narrates the very act of reading the holy texts as an exchange between Arab and Jew?

Know that if one does not understand the language of a human being whom one hears speaking, one indubitably knows that he speaks but without knowing what he intends to say. Something of even graver import may occur: sometimes one may hear in someone else's speech words that in the language of the speaker indicate a certain meaning and by accident that word indicates in the language of the hearer the contrary of what the speaker intended. Thus the hearer will think that the signification that the word has for the speaker is the same as its signification for him. For instance, if an Arab hears a Hebrew man saying 'aba, the Arab will think that he speaks of an individual who was reluctant with regard to some matter and refused (abâ) it. . . . This is similar to what happens with the multitude with regard to the speech of the prophets, excepting certain portions that they do not understand at all.[58]

6

What is the story, then, on the Jew, the Arab? What of narrative in Arab Jewish letters? Is narrative necessary? Does it enable a different framing of these questions as we have been addressing them? And when does the story end? When does "the classical" end? Does it, can it, should it ever end? Filiation and affiliation, the abandonment of the sons by the fathers, of the fathers by the sons, not to mention the women, mothers, sisters, and more, left behind or below, in Baghdad and elsewhere. Perhaps narrative itself should be abandoned. "What good were words? Disasters. Not since Rashid 'Ali had the Jews been in such panic. To leave, to leave."[59] To move again, as Shim'on Ballas, the author of the lines just quoted, does and explains, "I just moved from Arabic to Hebrew." To move at once further and closer, without certainty or clear consciousness, least of all one's own, but closer perhaps to yet another beginning, another narrative. "I think that I am probably trying to bring my Hebrew closer and closer to Arabic. This isn't done through syntax, but maybe through some sense of structure or way of approaching things. It is very abstract and I don't do it in a way that is completely conscious either. That's the problem, and it is extremely difficult to describe or quantify."[60] "If anything," Ballas continues, "I am in dialogue with language itself." In this dialogue there is hardly a sense of continuity, but narrative weaves continuity out of discontinuity and abandonment, beginning where there is no beginning, bridging that which cannot be bridged by telling a story.

The story is told:

> Tell me, you're from Israel?
> Yes, I'm from there.
> Oh and where in Israel do you live?
> Jerusalem. For the last few years I've lived there.
> Oh, Jerusalem is such a beautiful city.
> Yes, of course, a beautiful city.
> And do you . . . you're from West . . . or East . . . ?
> That's a tough question, depends on who's drawing the map.
> You're funny, and do you, I mean, do you speak Hebrew?
> Yes, of course.
> I mean, that's your mother tongue?
> No really. My mother's tongue is Arabic, but now she speaks
>   Hebrew fine.
> . . .
>
> Excuse me for prying, but I just have to ask you, are you Jewish
>   or Arab?
> I'm an Arab Jew.
> You're funny.[61]

The story and history of Arab Jewish relations rarely deals, as I have said, with narrative, and if with literature, mostly with poetry. There are exceptions, obviously, writers and scholars, and we have encountered some of them on the way. But some of the difficulties with which they, as well as we ourselves, struggle have to do with where to look for narrative and how to construct one (or many) out of those already existing. Between religion and literature, history and law, the history of scholarship regarding what Shlomo Goitein called "the Jewish-Arab symbiosis" has gone through a number of transformations that sought to determine the nature of the relations and distinctions, proximities and separations between Arabs and Jews, Jews and Muslims and lately Israelis and Palestinians.[62] Alternatively foregrounding race or culture, religion or ethnicity, language or law, they all participate in determining a priori that a bridge is missing. And a bridge *is* always missing, if not always where one thinks. This is one of the lessons of narrative, at least of didactic narrative. For whether found in poetry or in prose, whether in historical documents or anthropological ones,[63] philosophical allegories or kabbalistic "myth," criticism or literature, narrative cannot occur without the necessary possibility of relating that which lacks all relation, without the possibility and impossibility, without the necessity of, abandonment. Translation or conversion,[64] narrative begins there where there is no beginning, where there is and is not a beginning. As such (but there is no narrative as such), narrative is there to be excluded from or gathered in a book—and whether one or the other makes all the difference as the poorly chosen sons and daughters (and others) have found out often enough and continue to as I write. The book is not written, much less spoken, yet it is recited, repeated, and narrated, and there are many of its kind. In a way it is always "le même livre," at least in the sense that Abdelkebir Khatibi and Jacques Hassoun gave to the phrase when they sat down to write theirs.[65] Arab Jewish letters enable the assertion of filiation, the documentation and gathering of new narratives or collection of narratives, there where there are too many, or not enough, fathers and sons, sisters and mothers. And as we saw, filiations—narrative as genealogy, genealogy as narrative—are about beginnings (in Edward Said's sense of the term). They are about abandoning beginnings and beginnings as abandonment,[66] none of which are really (or fictionally) beginning anything. And perhaps they should teach us something—something about ends as well. But that may be going too far. At any rate, Arab Jewish letters, classical narratives if there are any, are about names and other language effects. Names such as Aïssa Josua, who in Edmond Amran El Maleh "declined his identity, as one says, in Arabic this lost and fully recovered language over the course of twenty years";[67] or "Mohammed Cohen," the character who gives his name to the title of another Arab Jewish novel written in French among the hundreds of such novels, also written in French (and, more recently, in Hebrew) by Maghrebian Jews over the course of the twentieth century, but it all began much before, and continued after, in France, Canada, or in Israel.[68] They are about exchanges, stories and histories, and jokes really, such as the following:

> Did you live in an Arab country?
> No, I am an Arab.
> Oh, I thought you were a Jew.
> Of course.
> Let me understand: Are you a Jew or an Arab.
> I am both.
> Half and half?
> No, entirely one and entirely the other.[69]

Within Arab Jewish letters, between Arabs and Jews, and perhaps most urgently, if more provincially, within Hebrew literature in its rapport to Arab literature, what such exchanges—between anything but two "sides"—what such narratives mean is that from now on, and from the beginning (only one beginning, but there is not one, that is, there is and there is not, if there has to be at all),

there has to be an Arab this time, as some sort of solution to some sort of silence. An Arab who speaks the language of Grace, as Dante once called it. Hebrew as the language of Grace, as opposed to the language of Confusion that swept over the world when the Tower of Babel collapsed. My Arab will build his tower of confusion on my plot. In the language of Grace. . . . I'll write about the loneliness of the Palestinian Arab Israeli, which is the greatest loneliness of all. With the skill of the veteran Samurai who is still remembered for a few precise and devastating sword strokes of prose, among the best in Hebrew literature.[70]

Notes

INTRODUCTION

1. Cotton Mather, "Letter to John Richards," in David Levin, *What Happened in Salem* (New York: Harcourt, Brace and World, 1960), 108. For this citation and interpretation of Mather and of the Salem trials I have relied on Nancy Ruttenburg, *Democratic Personality: Popular Voice and the Trial of American Authorship* (Stanford, CA: Stanford University Press, 1998), 1–82; on "the Reality of Invisibles" see esp. 63.

2. "The Return of Several Ministers Consulted," in Levin, *What Happened in Salem*, 110–111.

3. Talal Asad, "Conscripts of Western Civilization," in *Dialectical Anthropology: Essays in Honor of Stanley Diamond*, vol. 1., ed. Christine Ward Gailey (Gainesville: University Press of Florida, 1992), 333–351.

4. Max Horkheimer and Theodor Adorno, *Dialectic of Enlightenment: Philosophical Fragments*, trans. Edmund Jephcott (Stanford, CA: Stanford University Press, 2002), 154.

5. Ruttenburg, *Democratic Personality*, 6, 75.

6. For a discussion and critique of this famous phrase by J. R. Seeley see Nicolas B. Dirks, *Castes of Mind: Colonialism and the Making of Modern India* (Princeton, NJ: Princeton University Press, 2001), 303–315; see also Nicolas B. Dirks, *The Scandal of Empire: India and the Creation of Imperial Britain* (Cambridge, MA: Belknap Press of Harvard University Press, 2006). An illuminating discussion of continuities between the Spanish Empire and the British one can be found in Anthony Pagden, *Lords of All the World: Ideologies of Empire in Spain, Britain, and France, c. 1500–c. 1800* (New Haven, CT: Yale University Press, 1995).

7. Stathis Gourgouris, *Dream Nation: Enlightenment, Colonization, and the Institution of Modern Greece* (Stanford, CA: Stanford University Press, 1996), 163n5.

8. Ibid., 15.

9. Ibid., 39.

10. Ernest Renan, *De la part des peuples sémitiques dans l'histoire de la civilisation* (Paris: Michel Lévy Frères, 1875), 38–39 (this text was the 1862 inaugural lecture given by Renan upon assuming the Chair of Hebrew, Aramaic, and Syriac at the Collège de France). Sven Lindqvist's account of the "history of bombing" describes the significant, if by no means exclusive, role played by the Arab Muslim world—from Tripoli to Baghdad via Chechaouen (see Sven Lindqvist, *A History of Bombing*, trans. Linda Haverty Rugg [New York: New Press, 2001]).

11. The discussion on the importance of Edward Said's work for an understanding of Jewish and Zionist history was launched by Ella Shohat (see her *Taboo Memories, Diasporic Voices* [Durham, NC: Duke University Press, 2006]) and pursued by Ammiel Alcalay, *After Jews and Arabs: Remaking Levantine Culture* (Minneapolis: University of Minnesota Press, 1993) and Jonathan Boyarin, most particularly in his "The Missing Keyword: Reading Olender's Renan," in *Qui Parle* 7, no. 2 (spring/summer 1994): 43–56; as well as James Pasto, "Islam's 'Strange Secret Sharer': Orientalism, Judaism, and the Jewish Question," *Comparative Studies of Society and History* 40 (1998): 437–474; and Amnon Raz-Krakotzkin, "A Few Comments on Orientalism, Jewish Studies, and Israeli Society" [in Hebrew], *Jama'a* 3 (1998): 34–61; further elaborations can be found in the work of Susannah Heschel, Jonathan Hess, and Ivan Davidson Kalmar.

12. Asad, "Conscripts of Western Civilization," 333.

13. I am thinking here of the pathbreaking work of Maxime Rodinson and Edward Said but also of Abdelkebir Khatibi, Ella Shohat, Ammiel Alcalay, and others, who have maintained a discerning lens on the role (if never an absolute or exclusive one, of course) of Western agents when it comes to Jews and Arabs.

14. Talal Asad, *Genealogies of Religion: Discipline and Reasons of Power in Christianity and Islam* (Baltimore: Johns Hopkins University Press, 1993), 1; Talal Asad, *Formations of the Secular: Christianity, Islam, Modernity* (Stanford, CA: Stanford University Press, 2003), 5.

15. Ashis Nandy, *The Romance of the State and the Fate of Dissent in the Tropics* (New Delhi: Oxford University Press, 2003).

16. Amnon Raz-Krakotzkin, *Censorship, Editing, and the Text: Catholic Censorship and Hebrew Literature in the Sixteenth Century* [in Hebrew] (Jerusalem: Hebrew University Magness Press, 2005).

17. Tomoko Masuzawa, *The Invention of World Religions: Or, How European Universalism Was Preserved in the Language of Pluralism* (Chicago: University of Chicago Press, 2005).

CHAPTER I

1. Daniel Dubuisson phrases this in a different context: "In this universe of representations, each thing is at one and the same time constituted by everything that surrounds it and is itself constituent, since it is always capable of intervening in this environment by relocating or imperceptibly modifying itself. That is to say—and this is the essential point—no representation exists on its own in autonomous, unchanging fashion" (Daniel Dubuisson, *The Western Construction of Religion: Myths, Knowledge, and Ideology*, trans. William Sayers [Baltimore: Johns Hopkins University Press, 2003], 38–39). Strangely enough, this well-recognized lack of autonomy, the finitude of any system of representation, does not prevent Dubuisson from asserting the hermeticism of cultures. "Each of our worlds," he writes, "is closed in on itself, hermetically" (128). Given the epistemological limitations he himself describes, one might ask how such closure could be established, let alone verified.

2. This phrase and the argument I am attempting to paraphrase above are found in Jacques Derrida, "Signature, Event, Context," in *Margins of Philosophy*, trans. Alan Bass (Chicago: University of Chicago Press, 1982); see also Jacques Derrida, *Limited Inc.*, trans. Samuel Weber (Evanston, IL: Northwestern University Press, 1988). On Saussure see Jacques Derrida, *Of Grammatology*, trans. Gayatri C. Spivak (Baltimore: Johns Hopkins University Press, 1976).

3. Talal Asad, *Genealogies of Religion: Discipline and Reasons of Power in Christianity and Islam* (Baltimore: Johns Hopkins University Press, 1993), 27.

4. In *White Mythologies: Writing History and the West* (London: Routledge, 1994) Robert Young has probably gone the furthest in explicating that dimension of Derrida's work while engaging other critiques of modernity. It might be interesting, however, to conduct an empirical study addressing the way in which historians who claim to have unearthed some novelty are systematically criticized or undermined by those arguing, with no less documentation, that such presumed novelty is, in fact—in *historical* fact—older.

5. Considering the "new presence" that "man" is, Foucault writes of "the motive of this new presence, the modality proper to it, the particular arrangement of the *episteme* that justifies it, the new relation that is established by means of it between words, things, and their order" (Michel Foucault, *The Order of Things: An Archaeology of the Human Sciences* [New York: Vintage, 1973], 312).

6. In one of his striking formulations Derrida explains that "l'Un se garde de l'autre." "The One guards against/keeps for itself some of the other. It protects *itself* from the other, but in the movement of this jealous violence, it comprises in itself, thus guarding it, the self-otherness or self-difference (the difference from within oneself) which makes it One" (Jacques Derrida, *Archive Fever*, trans. Eric Prenowitz [Chicago: University of Chicago Press, 1998], 78, 84; see also Jacques

Derrida, *Politics of Friendship*, trans. George Collins [London: Verso, 1997]; and "Faith and Knowledge: The Two Sources of 'Religion' at the Limits of Reason Alone," trans. Samuel Weber, in Jacques Derrida, *Acts of Religion*, ed. Gil Anidjar [New York: Routledge, 2002], sec. 52).

7. I remain puzzled by the argument that "religion" can be isolated or bracketed as the identifiable culprit in what is wrong with political life, or even with the world or with humanity, today and since the beginning of history. Granting, for a moment, that religion would not only be violent, but disempowering, ideological, distracting, and de-responsibilizing; granted even that religion would *be* violence itself. Then what? That matters are more complicated is a banal understatement. For less banality on "violence and metaphysics" see Derrida's essay by that name in *Writing and Difference*, trans. Alan Bass (Chicago: University of Chicago Press, 1978); and, more recently, Jacques Derrida, *Without Alibi*, ed. and trans. Peggy Kamuf (Stanford, CA: Stanford University Press, 2002), esp. 238–280.

8. See Talal Asad's compelling argument that in order to describe a change in or of religion, "religion" has to remain "analytically identifiable." Something, an essence of religion, is said to remain the same *through* the historical change undergone *by* religion in "its social extension and function." Thus religion is seen as "a transhistorical and transcultural phenomenon" (Asad, *Genealogies of Religion*, 28). And compare Hans Kippenberg, who reinscribes the "passing away of religious traditions" that, occurring with modernization, would have led to the emergence of the discipline of comparative religion in the nineteenth century (Hans D. Kippenberg, *Discovering Religious History in the Modern Age*, trans. Barbara Harshav [Princeton, NJ: Princeton University Press, 2002], xi). Daniel Dubuisson has recently formulated a similar argument while focusing on the representational, psychical, and political investments at work in this essentialization (Dubuisson, *The Western Construction of Religion*). For my part I will do no more than try to follow as closely as possible the consequences of Asad's analyses for an understanding of "race and religion" or, as I will argue, Jews and Arabs.

9. Jonathan Z. Smith reinscribes in this territorial and proprietary fashion the quasi-divine sovereignty and creative power of the scholar, asserting that "religion" is "a term created by scholars for their intellectual purposes and therefore is theirs to define" (Jonathan Z. Smith, "Religion, Religions, Religious," in *Critical Terms for Religious Studies*, ed. Mark C. Taylor [Chicago: University of Chicago Press, 1998], 281). Responding to Smith by engaging the effects of "manufacturing religion" (partly following Noam Chomsky's "manufacturing consent"), Russell T. McCutcheon recalls that "scholars carry out their work in the sociohistorical world" and that the categories they employ and interrogate have "not only a history but also material implications" (Russell T. McCutcheon,

Manufacturing Religion [New York: Oxford University Press, 1997], x). Gavin Langmuir puts it in another, equally valid, way. Scholars of religion, he writes, "do not want to offend their many readers who belong to religions" (Gavin I. Langmuir, *History, Religion, and Antisemitism* [Berkeley: University of California Press, 1990], 5). This is not to preclude or even limit the possibilities of change but only to recognize that inventions occur under certain conditions.

10. William D. Hart, *Edward Said and the Religious Effects of Culture* (Cambridge, UK: Cambridge University Press, 2000).

11. On the importance of education and of mandatory schooling for a history of nationalism and racism see Etienne Balibar and Immanuel Wallerstein, *Race, nation, classe: Les identités ambiguës* (Paris: La découverte, 1997), esp. 117–143.

12. "On the one hand, Jewish social scientists were members of the general social scientific community. Educated in European universities, they spoke the language of European science; this was, by definition, the only language they could speak. On the other hand, they were Jews, engaged with their own community or people at both the intellectual and the practical level. This tension helped define Jewish social science to a significant degree" (Mitchell B. Hart, *Social Science and the Politics of Modern Jewish Identity* [Stanford, CA: Stanford University Press, 2000], 10). To the extent that, as Hart shows, social science "involved a reformulation of Jewish identity," to the extent that it involved "a refutation of the idea that Jewry (*Judentum*) could be 'reduced' or limited to religious identity and community," to the extent, finally, that Jews were being redefined by this new scientific discourse as "a *Volk* and a nation" (16), the dialectics of "resistance and rejection" as well as "acceptance and appropriation" that characterized the relation of Jews to anti-Semitism (12) are of extensive significance. Hence, the reach of Hart's argument goes well beyond the scientific discourse to which he attends in rigorous detail.

13. "Several historians, perhaps most notably Hannah Arendt, have distinguished sharply between the older hatred of Jews as religious and the modern hatred as secular (or racial)" (Langmuir, *History, Religion, and Antisemitism*, 10). I am not as certain as Langmuir appears to be of the popularity of Arendt's argument. Consider, for example, that Steven Aschheim, writing about the same period, describes it in precisely inverse terms. "Germany," Aschheim writes, "spearheaded the movement to dismiss the ethnic component of Jewish faith and to radically 'spiritualize' it" (Steven E. Aschheim, *Brothers and Strangers: The East European Jew in German and German Jewish Consciousness, 1800–1923* [Madison: University of Wisconsin Press, 1982], 16). Nor am I certain that Arendt's argument is altogether reducible to what Langmuir attributes to her.

14. "The theory that the Jews are always the scapegoat implies that the scapegoat might have been anyone as well. It upholds the perfect innocence of the

victim, an innocence which insinuates not only that no evil was done but that nothing at all was done which might possibly have a connection with the issue at stake" (Hannah Arendt, *The Origins of Totalitarianism* [New York: Meridian Books, 1958], 5). Arendt's words are increasingly pertinent in the current, reigning victimology.

15. Addressing another historical shift, which would separate "Judaism" and "Christianity" in early antiquity precisely in terms of ethnicity, race, and religion, Denise Kimber Buell has provocatively suggested that we begin thinking of "Christianness as a racial category." Buell is thus making the most compelling case to date for a rethinking of these categories. As Buell puts it, "[W]e have failed to recognize the importance and functions of ethnic reasoning in early Christian self-definition largely because of the way dominant *modern* ideas about race inform our approaches to and presuppositions about the meaning of race, ethnicity, and religion (including their possible relationships)" (Denise Kimber Buell, "Rethinking the Relevance of Race for Early Christian Self-Definition," *Harvard Theology Review* 94, no. 4 [2001]: 450). Implicitly offering an answer to the question "what the Christian wants," regarding a division of labor of sorts between religion and race, Buell elsewhere explains that "any evidence for early Christian self-definition in terms of 'peoplehood,' 'family,' and 'kinship,' is interpreted as metaphoric, implying that when other groups use such concepts they mean them 'literally.' This framing makes race seem irrelevant for describing a historical movement constituted by means of joining. But if we view both race and religion as socially and historically contingent concepts with no essential meanings or intrinsic relationship with one another, then we must not read early Christian literature through a lens that presumes a disjuncture between Christianness and race (or kinship)" (Denise Kimber Buell, "Race and Universalism in Early Christianity," *Journal of Early Christian Studies* 10, no. 4 [2002]: 436).

16. I have learned much from Maurice Olender's study, which documents this invention in numerous, and nuanced, ways. Unlike Said, however, Olender only marginally alludes to the discursive collusion that links the scholars he discusses to the history of imperialism, indeed, to the specificity of Orientalism in the colonial history of the West. In this context it is perhaps interesting to consider the translation of Olender's title, particularly since the book has recently been published again in English. The original French title is *Les langues du paradis. Aryens et Sémites: Un couple providentiel* (Paris: Gallimard/Seuil, 1989). The 1992 translation by Arthur Goldhammer bears the title *The Languages of Paradise: Race, Religion, and Philology in the Nineteenth Century* (Cambridge, MA: Harvard University Press, 1992), whereas the recent version—by the same translator, only a different publisher—has a more accurate, if more concealing, ren-

dering: *The Languages of Paradise: Aryans and Semites, a Match Made in Heaven* (New York: Other Press, 2002). The argument remains the same, obviously, and it engages, crucially, both race and religion.

17. On the Hamitic hypothesis see Mahmood Mamdani, *When Victims Become Killers: Colonialism, Nativism, and the Genocide in Rwanda* (Princeton, NJ: Princeton University Press, 2001).

18. The historical method—if there is one—deployed by Lewis in his discussion of "Semites and anti-Semites" remains quite baffling (see Bernard Lewis, *Semites and Anti-Semites: An Inquiry into Conflict and Prejudice* [New York: Norton, 1999]). Hence, whereas he correctly points out that both Aryans and Semites are mythical figures ("Both of them are myths, and part of the same mythology" [43]), derivative, moreover, of the modern invention of comparative philology ("Both names have their origin in scholarship and refer to language. Both date from the great development of comparative philology in the late eighteenth and early nineteenth centuries" [43]), Lewis nonetheless introduces the Semites by way of a narrative going back to ancient peoples invoked in the biblical texts as if there were, in this remote context, any historical relevance to the category of "Semites." Lewis goes on to underscore the linguistic dimension of the category "Semite," as well as the erroneous, even obsolete, but to his mind apparently quite benign, conceptions of race operative in the nineteenth century ("At one time, [the term *Semitic*] might thus have had a connotation of race, when that word itself was used to designate national and cultural entities. It has nothing whatever to do with race in the anthropological sense that is now common usage" [45]). Later on Lewis will go so far as to argue that "the term 'Semite' has no meaning when applied to groups as heterogeneous as the Arabs or the Jews" (117), a declaration that would lead one to dismiss as gibberish the libraries (including Lewis's own books) that claim meaningful expertise on precisely such groups in their entirety (an expertise that I myself do not particularly seek to validate either way). But Lewis's agenda is here different, especially when he finally admits that there are lingering effects to "linguistic" scholarship. Lewis mostly means to cast doubt on the notion that in the development of Semitics there was any racism involved (any racism, that is, directed at anyone but Jews). For if "indeed it could be argued that the use of such terms is in itself a sign of racism and certainly of either ignorance or bad faith," one thing remains certain and beyond what is otherwise no more than a hypothetical argument: "Anti-Semitism has never anywhere been concerned with anyone but Jews" (117). Bad faith, indeed. And poor historical work.

19. See Joseph Massad, "The Ends of Zionism: Racism and the Palestinian Struggle," *Interventions: International Journal of Postcolonial Studies* 5, no. 3 (2003): 440–451. In France the discrepancy could be explored around the use of

expressions referring to individuals "issus de l'immigration" or to "maghrébins," which are only invoked when speaking about Arabs and Muslims. The large majority of French Jews, who arrived in France as a result of the same immigration, out of the same Maghrebian countries, are apparently completely different.
 20. Adolf Hitler, *Mein Kampf,* trans. Ralph Manheim (Cambridge, MA: Riverside Press, 1962), 150; and further: "The Jew has always been a people with definite racial characteristics and never a religion" [306]). Later on, Hitler will claim that the Jews use religion to occlude their racial identity. The Jews' "whole existence is based on one single great lie, to wit, that they are a religious community while actually they are a race" (232). Significantly, Hitler credits the Zionists for publicly acknowledging, at least, the Jews' racial-national identity (56). Hitler also fails the Zionists for their attempt at making the world believe they would be satisfied with the creation of a state (325). It is a puzzling fact of scholarship that, to my knowledge at least, the research done on Nazi science and doctrine has refrained from engaging the specific and common heritage of philological and racial studies conducted on "Semites" (and, more specifically, Arabs and Muslims) in Germany and elsewhere over the course of the nineteenth century and early twentieth (although clearly the philological and theological heritage is being recognized, as has recently been argued by Richard Steigmann-Gall, *The Holy Reich: Nazi Conceptions of Christianity, 1919–1945* [Cambridge, UK: Cambridge University Press, 2003], esp. 108 for a discussion of Renan). Most striking in this context is the overwhelming absence of interest in the Muslim, the "Muselmann" of concentration camps (as well as an early name of the first non-Aryan division of the Waffen-SS), and more generally in the Nazi attitudes and theorizations regarding Arabs and Muslims. In my own discussion of the "Muslims" I remarked that the meager scholarship on the Nazis and the Arabs has remained focused on foreign policy rather than on racial doctrine and policies. Following Primo Levi, if for different reasons from those on which he elaborated, it seems to me crucial to recognize the epochal significance of the figure of the "Muslims" and quite precisely so for an understanding of the relation between race and religion, the Jew, the Arab (see Gil Anidjar, *The Jew, the Arab: A History of the Enemy* [Stanford, CA: Stanford University Press, 2003], esp. 229n113). I should also mention that the work of Gerhard Höpp, of which I learned all too late, is devoted to the question of Muslim presence in Germany and German writing and scholarship. In a series of articles published just before his death, Höpp engaged the question of Arabs and Muslims in concentration camps in the context of Nazi racial policy. What he shows, aside from the dearth of scholarship, is the strange vanishing of racial thought on the part of the Nazis when it came to Arabs and Muslims. The Arabs did belong to the Semitic race but were distinguished from the Jews in numerous ways (see Gerhard Höpp,

"'Gefährdungen der Erinnerung': Arabische Häftlinge in Nationalsozialistischen Konzentrationslagern," *Asien afrika lateinamerika* 30 [2002]: 373–386; and "Im Schatten des Mondes. Arabische Opfer des Nationalsozialismus," *Sozial Geschichte Zeitschrift für historische Analyse des 20. Jahrhunderts* 2 [2002]; see also the work of Ekkehard Ellinger, who reviews the historical sources concerning German Orientalism—Orientalistik and Semitistik—during the Nazi regime [Ekkehard Ellinger, "Deutschsprachige Orientalistik zur Zeit des Nationalsozialismus, 1933–1945," master's thesis, Freie Universität, Berlin, April 1998]. I am grateful to Georges Khalil for directing me to both Höpp's and Ellinger's work).

21. Consider Hitler's recognition of (and implicit admiration for) Islam's efficiency in spreading its doctrine when comparing it with the Christian missionary movement (Hitler, *Mein Kampf,* 267). Aside from this I could not find any other references to Islam or to Arabs in *Mein Kampf.* One further remark on the matter: the dearth of scholarship on Nazism and Islam and the Arabs is perhaps comparable to the lack of attention given to blacks in the same context. In a recent study Clarence Lusane points out that "Afro-Germans, and Blacks in general" have been massively under-studied. It is important to note that, over against Muslims and Arabs, blacks were repeatedly "vilified by the Nazi leadership as exemplified throughout Hitler's *Mein Kampf.*" Lusane demonstrates the importance of microanalysis of race policies when he shows, for example, that blacks in Nazi Germany were stigmatized and victimized, brutalized, sterilized, and imprisoned, even killed but "were never named as a group to be gathered up and dealt with by physical elimination" (Clarence Lusane, *Hitler's Black Victims: The Historical Experiences of Afro-Germans, European Blacks, Africans, and African Americans in the Nazi Era* [New York: Routledge, 2003], 98, 181).

22. In their discussion of "the Racial State" Burleigh and Wippermann make no mention of Arabs or Semites, although they demonstrate how wide-ranging was the scientific and political reach of Nazi racism (Michael Burleigh and Wolfgang Wippermann, *The Racial State: Germany, 1933–1945* [Cambridge, UK: Cambridge University Press, 1991]). Let me emphasize that I have little patience for the still current and persistent obsession with the Mufti of Jerusalem or for claims about alliances between Nazis and Arabs. As Lukasz Hirszowicz explains, Arabs were on the lowest rungs of Hitler's racial ladder (consider the example of the Moor as helping beast to be dispensed with as technology develops in *Mein Kampf,* 294 [Lukasz Hirszowicz, *The Third Reich and the Arab East* (London: Routledge and Kegan Paul, 1966), 315]), a fact that, as with the Jews, does not preclude contamination and therefore holds little critical potential. Clearly, foreign policy (especially against the colonial interests of England) was determining the moves of the Nazi State, but it does not suffice by way of explanation for

what is "domestically," one might say, mostly a lack of investment. Consider further that Hans Günther, holder of the chair of "racial science" at Jena under the Nazis, wrote that "in view of the large variety of human types among the peoples of the Semitic languages, how could one speak of a 'Semitic race'?" (H. F. K. Günther, "The Nordic Race as 'Ideal Type,'" in George L. Mosse, *Nazi Culture: Intellectual, Cultural, and Social Life in the Third Reich* [New York: Grosset and Dunlap, 1973], 61). There still remains, therefore, the puzzle of how to account for the disappearance of the Semite for these proud "Aryans," the disappearance, more precisely, of the Arab after the achievements of scientific doctrines establishing the existence of a race of Aryans and doing so by equating, on the opposite side, both Jew and Arab under the figure of the Semite.

23. Arendt, *Origins of Totalitarianism*, 239, 290. And see her critique of Zionism in Hannah Arendt, *The Jew as Pariah: Jewish Identity and Politics in the Modern Age*, ed. Ron H. Feldman (New York: Grove Press, 1978).

24. On American Jews see Karen Brodkin, *How Jews Became White Folks and What That Says About Race in America* (New Brunswick, NJ: Rutgers University Press, 1999). On Israel/Palestine see Ella Shohat, *Israeli Cinema: East/West and the Politics of Representation* (Austin: University of Texas Press, 1988); and Joseph Massad, "Palestinians and the Limits of Racialized Discourse," *Social Text* 34 (spring 1993): 94–114; see also Joseph Massad, "The 'Post-Colonial' Colony: Time, Space, and Bodies in Palestine/Israel," in *The Pre-Occupation of Postcolonial Studies*, ed. Fawzia Afzal-Khan and Kalpana Seshadri-Crooks (Durham, NC: Duke University Press, 2000), 311–346.

25. Amnon Raz-Krakotzkin, "Orientalism, Jewish Studies, and Israeli Society: A Few Considerations" [in Hebrew], *Jama'a* 3, no. 1 (1999): 34–59, esp. 48; see also Menahem Milson, who describes the School of Oriental Studies as "one of the first components of the Hebrew University of Jerusalem . . . founded in 1926 and, in the field of Humanities, was preceded only by the Institute of Jewish Studies, which opened its doors in December 1924" (Menahem Milson, "The Beginnings of Arabic and Islamic Studies at the Hebrew University of Jerusalem," *Judaism* 45, no. 2 [spring 1996]: 169). Justifiably lamenting the lack of studies on the history of "Semitics" and, indeed, of a crucial chapter in German Orientalism, Ludmila Hanisch traces the development and separation of the study of Judaism from that of "Semitics" in Nazi Germany, asserting that during the Third Reich "the study of Jewish religion, history and culture became a special branch." To this day "it is no longer part of Oriental studies" (Ludmila Hanisch, "Akzentverschiebung—Zur Geschichte der Semitistik und Islamwissenschaft während des 'Dritten Reichs,'" *Berichte zur Wissenschaftsgeschichte* 18 [1995]: 217–226). Today the Hebrew University distinguishes in its departments between the "ancient Middle East," "Islam and the Middle East," and "Asia

and Africa Studies," all of which are, as Raz-Krakotzkin has shown, distinct from "General History" (the history of the West) and from "Jewish History" and "Jewish Studies." Such separations are now typical in the United States as well, although their persistent interrogation (and inertia) may have brought about some limited changes (or lingering effects).

26. One could point to a recent example of scholarship that, rigorous and innovative, also maintains the same divisions between Jews and Arabs, between anti-Semitism and colonialism, between religion and race, precisely when articulating the shifts between one and the other. In his important book, *Germans, Jews, and the Claims of Modernity*, Jonathan Hess acknowledges the governing effects of Orientalism (as theorized by Edward Said). Clearly, Hess is quite right when he asserts that in the eighteenth century Johann David Michaelis was "more Eurocentric than his nineteenth-century successors in Semitic studies, concerned more with ancient Israelites and modern Jews than with Arabs, whom he reduces to sources of potential data for the historical study of the Hebrew Bible. Islam is of little concern to him" (Jonathan M. Hess, *Germans, Jews, and the Claims of Modernity* [New Haven, CT: Yale University Press, 2002], 57). It is with this lack of concern, and from this discrepancy in emotional investment (if not in scholarly interest), that one can further appreciate Hess's careful reflections. Why is it that, if Jews and Arabs are seen as one and the same object of study ("The nomadic Arabs, conveniently enough, have apparently remained trapped in the state of childhood Michaelis saw as characteristic of the ancient Israelites" [63]), one group is considered less (or, in other cases, more) important? Beyond individual preferences and even programmatic politics, what are the mechanisms that insist on the distinction at the very same moment that distinction is otherwise abolished? To be sure, one wonders whether the distinct focus Hess argues for is Michaelis's own or the continued effect of a history that remains invisible. Indeed, Hess rightly points out that "for Michaelis, modern Arabs are the *only* legitimate descendants of the ancient Israelites" (67; emphasis added). For Michaelis, then, the modern Jews are not Arab enough, yet perhaps they should be. The collapse of a distinction between them is a *desideratum* if not a given. Hess painstakingly documents the ongoing resistances to this collapse, bringing about a much keener understanding of "the Specter of Racial Antisemitism" (as the subtitle of his chapter has it). Lingering on the chosenness of the Jews as quasi-exclusive targets of the new racism that was emerging in German culture, Hess significantly advances our understanding of a larger complex of investments and denegations, all of which are at work at the very moment "modernity" and with it the Semites (Jews and Arabs) emerge out of Europe's consciousness.

27. Ernest Renan, *Etudes d'histoire religieuse* (Paris: Gallimard, 1992), 65.

28. See Richard King's discussion of these issues in *Orientalism and Religion: Postcolonial Theory, India, and "The Mystic East"* (London: Routledge, 1999). On Marx and the "history of religions" see Rosalind C. Morris, "Theses on the Question of War: History, Media, Terror," *Social Text* 20, no. 3 (fall 2002): 149–175.

29. I quote here from William Hart, *Edward Said and the Religious Effects of Culture* (Cambridge, UK: Cambridge University Press, 2000), 83.

30. Yosef Hayim Yerushalmi has interrogated the "modernity," indeed, the cooperation (collaboration?), of periodization with categories such as religion and race in the case of biological racism (here defined narrowly as the attribution of immutability to certain "genetic" traits of a given group). Yerushalmi points out that some kind of genetic conceptions were at work before modern times, before "secularization," which hold easily recognizable characteristics of modern racism. Clearly, immutability is not the privilege of modern racism (or, for that matter, of biological thinking). Yet Yerushalmi admittedly writes of a period when the very distinction between religion and race was not yet established, let alone recognized. The lack of a discursive regime whereby "race" is isolated, distinguished from "religion," and in which it becomes a governing principle explicitly contrasted with religion grounds the specificity of "modern racism" (see Yosef Hayim Yerushalmi, *Sefardica* [Paris: Chandeigne, 1998], 255–292). Note, for example, that the "drop of blood" theory elaborated by Fray Francisco de Torrejoncillo affirms that such "contamination" finds confirmation in the "judaizing" tendencies of "infected persons." What the blood carries and preserves, in other words, is still what we would call "religion." Not so with the Nazis.

31. Mitchell B. Hart, *Social Science and the Politics of Modern Jewish Identity* (Stanford, CA: Stanford University Press, 2000).

32. Freud, quoted in Sander L. Gilman, *Freud, Race, and Gender* (Princeton, NJ: Princeton University Press, 1993), 35.

33. On the "third sex" see ibid., 47; see also Daniel Boyarin, *Unheroic Conduct: The Rise of Heterosexuality and the Invention of the Jewish Man* (Berkeley: University of California Press, 1997).

34. As Mitchell Hart explains, "the denial by Zionism of the solely religious character of Jewry, and the attempt to redefine Jewry along national/racial lines, were anathema to the majority of Jews" (Hart, *Social Science*, 46). On the invention of Judaism as religion see Susannah Heschel, *Abraham Geiger and the Jewish Jesus* (Chicago: University of Chicago Press, 1998). Jonathan Hess corroborates Heschel's argument, writing that "Judaism as a 'religion' is a distinctly modern invention developed in mimicry of Christianity; premodern Jewish texts typically speak of Torah and *mitzvot* but rarely present Judaism as a religion in any way similar to Christianity" (Hess, *Germans, Jews, and the Claims of Modernity*,

96). Moses Mendelssohn was, according to Hess, instrumental in promoting the adoption of this new conception of Judaism. It was a polemical conception, one explicitly meant to oppose the anti-Jewish prejudice that was "a crucial component of modern Orientalist scholarship, central to the way in which Europeans had recently come to conceive of the Jews' Oriental heritage" (106). It is primarily "Michaelis's presentation of Judaism as an 'Oriental' legal system" that "clearly lurks in the background of [Mendelssohn's] *Jerusalem*, ultimately providing the antithesis of Mendelssohn's vision of Diaspora. Judaism for Mendelssohn is neither 'Oriental' nor European" (97). Although religion and the Orient will not stay distinct for long, the important point is that the two notions emerge together. Consciously invoking a somehow anachronistic terminology, Miriam Bodian documents the first signs of this contemporary emergence when she writes of the adoption, by Portuguese Jews such as Menasseh ben Israel, of notions akin to the infamous Spanish "purity of blood" and the ensuing "distinction between religious and ethnic affiliation." "It is striking," Bodian writes, "to find such a distinction . . . among seventeenth century Jews. Indeed, more than a century would pass before European Jews, pressured by demands to demonstrate *national allegiance*, would begin actively to confine their Jewish affiliation to the sphere of religion" (Miriam Bodian, *Hebrews of the Portuguese Nation: Conversos and Community in Early Modern Amsterdam* [Bloomington: Indiana University Press, 1997], 153; emphasis added). By then, "national allegiance" will hardly be distinguishable from "ethnicity" or from "religion," however secularized. Significantly, Bodian also writes of the becoming-religion of the Jews at the same time, and at the hands of none other than Napoleon: "Powerful political forces were pressuring Jewish communities throughout Europe to relinquish their judicial and civil powers and become religious institutions with limited functions. Napoleon struck the first decisive blow," first in France, then in the Netherlands (159).

35. I borrow the phrase "disciplinary revolution" from Philip S. Gorski's provocative *The Disciplinary Revolution: Calvinism and the Rise of the State in Early Modern Europe* (Chicago: University of Chicago Press, 2003).

36. Spinoza, *Theologico-Political Treatise*, trans. R. H. M. Elwes (New York: Dover, 1951), 17.

37. According to Kant

> [t]he Palestinians living among us have, for the most part, earned a not unfounded reputation for being cheaters, because of their spirit of usury since their exile. Certainly, it seems strange to conceive of a *nation* of cheaters (*eine* Nation *von Betrügern*); but it is just as odd to think of a nation of merchants (*eine Nation von lauter Kaufleuten*), the great majority of whom, bound by an ancient superstition that is recognized by the State

they live in, seek no civil dignity (*keine bürgerliche Ehre sucht*) and try to make up for this loss by the advantage of duping the people among whom they find refuge, and even one another. The situation could not be otherwise, given a whole nation of merchants, as non-productive members of society (for examples, the Jews in Poland). So their constitution (*Verfassung*), which is sanctioned by ancient precepts and even by the people among whom they live (since we have certain sacred writings in common with them), cannot consistently be abolished—even though the supreme principle of their morality in trading with us is "Let the buyer beware."— I shall not engage in the futile undertaking of lecturing to these people (*dieses Volk*), in terms of morality, about cheating and honesty. Instead, I shall present my conjectures about the origin of this peculiar constitution (the constitution, namely, of a nation of merchants).

There follows Kant's "conjectures," which are, for the most part, about geographical migratory movements since at least King Solomon. Kant then proceeds toward a conclusion of sorts to this matter: "So their dispersal throughout the world, with their union in religion and language (*in Religion und Sprache*), cannot be attributed to a *curse* that befell this people (*dieses Volk*). It must rather be considered a *blessing*, especially since their *per capita* wealth is probably greater than that of any other people (*eines jeden anderen Volks*) of the same number" (Immanuel Kant, *Anthropology from a Pragmatic Point of View*, trans. Mary J. Gregor [The Hague: Martinus Nijhoff, 1974], sec. 46, 77n). Further on, in his discussion of the "character of nations," Kant will not revisit this peculiar "nation of merchants," nor do the Jews appear in Kant's discussions of the races of humankind.

38. I am referring to Marx's "On the Jewish Question," which may echo Voltaire's hilarious, if mean-spirited, treatment of the most singular "nation juive," in his *Dictionaire philosophique* (art. "Juifs"), where he castigates (among other things) the theological inabilities of the Jews (in fact, their complete inaptitude at being original in any way), only to praise their mercantile intelligence. Voltaire recognizes that Jews have been persecuted, and he blatantly blames the victims, but not *only* the victims.

39. For a discussion of the "substrate" as an archival problem see Derrida, *Archive Fever*.

40. Hannah Arendt, *Eichmann in Jerusalem: A Report on the Banality of Evil* (New York: Penguin, 1994), 259.

41. Hannah Arendt, "On Humanity in Dark Times: Thoughts About Lessing," trans. Clara Winston and Richard Winston, in *Men in Dark Times* (New York: Harcourt Brace Jovanovich, 1968), 18.

42. Smith, "Religion, Religions, Religious," 269. For an extensive discussion

of the change jointly undergone by Christianity and Judaism, as categories such as religion and literature, race and ethnicity, and, indeed, "Judaism" and "Christianity" are beginning to be elaborated, see Amnon Raz-Krakotzkin, *The Censor, the Editor, and the Text: Catholic Censorship and Hebrew Literature in the Sixteenth Century* (Philadelphia: University of Pennsylvania Press, forthcoming).

43. Frank E. Manuel, *The Eighteenth Century Confronts the Gods* (Cambridge, MA: Harvard University Press, 1959), 6.

44. On the importance of the nineteenth century in Europe and America as to the validation and institutionalization of a distinct field of study entitled "religion," and precisely in relation to Western colonialism, that is to say, to racism and to imperialism, "the global mentality of colonialism," see John P. Burris, *Exhibiting Religion: Colonialism and Spectacle at International Expositions, 1851–1893* (Charlottesville: University Press of Virginia, 2001).

45. Gustavo Benavides, "Modernity," in *Critical Terms for Religious Studies*, ed. Mark C. Taylor (Chicago: University of Chicago Press, 1998), 193. The distinction between religion and race is briefly invoked by Smith himself, who recalls, while engaging the American scholar W. D. Whitney, the short-lived notion of "race religion" (to be distinguished, according to Whitney, from religions brought about by the actions of an individual founder). The difficulty that surrounds "Judaism" in Whitney's scheme, Smith writes, "makes clear the dilemma posed by the study of the 'religions' from the perspective of the spiritual" (277).

46. Denise K. Buell, "Rethinking the Relevance of Race for Early Christian Self-Definition," *Harvard Theological Review* 94, no. 4 (2001): 449, 452.

47. Once again, I refer the reader to Denise Buell's work on these issues.

48. Clearly, Homi Bhabha is right to describe the Bible as an "English book," as he is no doubt correct to point out that "the natives resist the miraculous equivalence of God and the English." In order to assert, however, that what the colonizers were trying to do to the natives was "to lessen their dependence on their own religious and cultural traditions," one needs to wonder—signs taken for wonders—about the apparently seamless transformations of the English book from the Bible into Conrad and Naipaul. One needs to wonder, in other words, about "religion" (Homi K. Bhabha, "Signs Taken for Wonders: Questions of Ambivalence and Authority Under a Tree Outside Delhi, May 1817," in *"Race," Writing, and Difference*, ed. Henry Louis Gates Jr. [Chicago: University of Chicago Press, 1986], 178–179).

49. Peter Harrison, *"Religion" and the Religions in the English Enlightenment* (Cambridge, UK: Cambridge University Press, 1990), 174.

50. Jonathan Z. Smith and Russell McCutcheon (and others as well) advance similar arguments regarding the "division of labor" between language (or area studies) departments and religion departments. As will become clear, how-

ever, I do not think that "the study of religion literally deconstructs itself into unrelated area studies," nor do I think that "the pie" of humanistic studies in the university is simply cut up according to functional or heuristic principles (see McCutcheon, *Manufacturing Religion*, 204, 224n7). McCutcheon's analysis, otherwise so trenchant, falls short here when he fails to address in depth the arguably epiphenomenal fact that the writings of Edward Said "are often overlooked by scholars of religion" (189). It is less an issue of whether "nationalism is a religion" than of what enables the two to be construed as so distant that they hardly deserve sustained common study. There is more than a matter of disagreement as to methods and conceptions of power; indeed, there is a series of invisible mechanisms that effectively separate religion and race (and consider, a few pages earlier, the absence of any query or reflection, on McCutcheon's part, as to the place and role of "religion" in David Theo Goldberg's description of "the modern discourse on race" (181–182). McCutcheon is clearly and laudably concerned with the racism at work in religious studies, but he does not engage the multiple discursive links between religion and race. More and more scholars have been arguing for a rapprochement between religious studies and cultural studies, for a substitution, as it were, of religion with culture (compelling instances of this argument can be found in King, *Orientalism and Religion*; and in Timothy Fitzgerald, *The Ideology of Religious Studies* [New York: Oxford University Press, 2000]). Be the value of such change what it may, it would also have to contend with the all-too-sedimented distinction (and lack thereof) between race and culture, and race and religion. For my part I do not mean to suggest that religious studies should retire quietly ("it does not thereby reduce itself, *ipso facto*, to the status of an imposture" as Foucault put it (see Foucault, *The Order of Things*, 365) but rather to argue that the two categories (race and religion) are discursively co-constitutive, that they operate in concert (regardless of intentionality), particularly where one appears to be irrelevant to the other.

51. John Burris spends some time discussing the generalization of divisions "between 'primitive' and 'civilized' peoples," divisions that "resulted in peoples deemed primitive becoming defined predominantly by cultural affiliation, or 'race,' as opposed to 'religion.'" As a consequence these groups "became usurped under the aegis of anthropological studies—as cultural rather than religious 'specimens.'" Burris thus pointedly argues that "the concept 'religion' can be seen as reinforcing colonial categories rather than acting as a point of critique of them" (Burris, *Exhibiting Religion*, xix). Native Americans, for example, "had come to be identified more by ethnicity than by religion" (126). Thus they became objects of the equally young discipline of anthropology. Howard Eilberg-Schwarz describes the comparatively recent shift undergone by Judaism in precisely those terms, which may be considered a turn as well as a return. It is a turn

to the extent that, under the influence of Edmund Leach and Mary Douglas, Judaism finally became an anthropological object, whereas it had been maintained within the domain of (advanced) "religion." Eilberg-Schwartz's compelling narrative would have to be qualified and recast as a return to the extent that it also corresponds to the ethnicization of the Jews, an issue that is becoming more recognizable in American academic discourse and that includes the Jews in novel ways within the study of American ethnicity. Reviving some of the gestures of Orientalism and race theory, and sustaining in some measure the racist discourse of the state of Israel, the "savage in Judaism" is thus also a reincarnation, not quite a novelty. This makes more sense if one recognizes the determining role of the emerging disciplines (anthropology and the study of religion) in the construction of both race and religion—in the invention of the Semites—in the nineteenth century (H. Eilberg-Schwartz, *The Savage in Judaism: An Anthropology of Israelite Religion and Ancient Judaism* [Bloomington: Indiana University Press, 1990]).

52. By *co-concealing* I mean to follow on what David Theo Goldberg calls "the masks of race," arguing that religion is one of those masks rather than a preexisting background to modern racism or simply one of the constitutive elements in what became racial or ethnic identity (see David Theo Goldberg, *Racist Culture: Philosophy and the Politics of Meaning* [Oxford: Basil Blackwell, 1993], esp. 61–89).

53. I borrow the term *excision* from Sander Gilman, who writes that "the rhetoric of race was excised from Freud's scientific writing and appeared only in his construction of gender" (Gilman, *Freud, Race, and Gender*, 37).

54. In 2002, faced with irresolvable conflicts that followed the massive influx of immigrants from the former Soviet Union (conflicts that involved the State bureaucracy, including the Rabbinate and its concern over "proper" Jewishness), the Israeli legislature abolished the category of "nationality" from Israeli ID cards. There are other state and cultural apparatuses, of course, that effectively maintain divisions that have long been sedimented into Israeli discourse and society.

55. Hart, *Social Science*, 46.

56. Lewis, *Semites and Anti-Semites*, 34.

57. Edward W. Said, *Orientalism* (New York: Vintage, 1979), 115, 102; for a discussion of the Semites, most specifically in the context of Ernest Renan's work, see *Orientalism*, 130–148.

58. Olender, *The Languages of Paradise*, 15 (translation altered).

59. Arendt, *Origins of Totalitarianism*, 174. Edward Said's account of Renan's work and importance remains as acute and as necessary today as it was when he wrote *Orientalism*. William Hart explains that, for Said, Renan should be

understood in rigorous Foucauldian terms, as one of the modern "founders of discursivity" (Hart, *Edward Said*, 67).

60. Renan, *Etudes d'histoire religieuse*, 86.

61. Heschel, *Abraham Geiger*, 156. William Hart concurs in his description that the racial distinction between Aryans and Semites is "integrally connected to invidious distinctions between religious traditions, between Christians and Jews and between Christians and Muslims." Hart is therefore right to conclude that "the important thing to ponder now are the fluid relations between Orientalism, racial thinking, and invidious religious distinctions" (Hart, *Edward Said*, 22–23). Surprisingly, even though he knows that "Islam as an object of discourse, and certainly as a proper name, is a rather late development" and that it has become "primarily an object of a Christian and Western discourse called religion," Hart nonetheless reinscribes the distinction between religion and race as subsequent effects of history rather than as contemporary, co-concealing disciplinary mechanisms (84–85). It is thus not only, not primarily, for Edward Said that "Religion and secularism are East and West" but indeed for a perspective that sees itself as "enlightened, rational, nondogmatic, secular (European!)" (86). Rather than criticize the very distinction, Hart enigmatically chooses to "locate" Said's "cultural common sense" and asserts that he is "not disposed to be too critical" of epistemic circumstances he otherwise diagnoses (87).

62. William Robertson Smith, *The Religion of the Semites* (New Brunswick, NJ: Transaction, 2002), 20.

63. Having asserted the linguistic and racial unity of the Semites, it is indeed with religion that Robertson Smith rounds off his claim to their unity and integrity, not to mention their stagnation, of course. "Thus, the whole course of history, from the earliest date to which authentic knowledge extends down to the time of the decay of the Caliphate, records no great permanent disturbance of population to affect the constancy of the Semitic type within its original seats" (Robertson Smith, *Religion of the Semites*, 12). It is this lack of change, "these widespread and permanent features," that arouses the interest in Semitic religion. Moreover, "it was in them and not in the things that vary from place to place and from time to time, that the strength of Semitic religion lay" (15). Such stagnating capacities will render much easier an inquiry into "the earlier faith of the race" (ibid.). Said highlights the way in which religion is here nonetheless (if ambivalently) valorized in order to dismiss the race. Said quotes Smith, who writes that it is "a great fault of the religion of the Prophet that it lends itself so easily to the prejudices of the race among whom it was first promulgated" (quoted in Said, *Orientalism*, 236). It will be recalled that Robertson Smith was an important source for Freud's argument (Freud refers to him as "a man of genius" in *Moses and Monotheism*). In fact, Freud underscores the complexities

of the matter as I merely broach them here. Dedicating his entire *Moses and Monotheism* to the question of "religion" and to the Jewish religion in particular, Freud both maintains the conflation of race and religion (insisting, in the process, on the virility of the Semites) and struggles against the imminent disappearance of the Semites (as either race or religion). But the rift has been opened. Hence, "the Jewish people under Moses were just as little able to tolerate such a highly spiritualized religion . . . as had been the Egyptians of the Eighteenth Dynasty. The same thing happened in both cases: those who had been dominated and kept in want rose and threw off the burden of the religion that had been imposed on them. But while the tame Egyptians waited till fate had removed the sacred figure of their Pharaoh, the savage Semites took fate into their own hands and rid themselves of their tyrant" (Sigmund Freud, *Moses and Monotheism*, in *The Standard Edition of the Complete Psychological Works of Sigmund Freud*, ed. James Strachey [London: Hogarth Press and the Institute of Psycho-Analysis, 1964], 23:47).

64. Renan, *Histoire générale et système comparé des langues sémitiques* (Paris: Calmann Lévy, 1877), 4.

65. Renan, *Etudes d'histoire religieuse*, 86.

66. Quoted in M. Olender, *Languages of Paradise*, 81; and compare Robertson Smith's claim for a kind of spontaneous generation. "Judaism, Christianity and Islam," he writes, "are *positive religions*, that is, they did not grow up like the systems of ancient heathenism, under the action of unconscious forces operating silently from age to age, but trace their origin to the teaching of great religious innovators, who spoke as the organs of a divine revelation, and deliberately departed from the traditions of the past." Still, there is some inheritance, which had been gathered by "successive generations of the Semitic race" and into which it "grew up as it were *instinctively*" (William Robertson Smith, *The Religion of the Semites*, 1–2; emphasis added).

67. In "What Is a Nation" Renan famously elaborates on his ambivalent attitude toward racial discourse (see Ernest Renan, "What Is a Nation," trans. Martin Thom, in *Nation and Narration*, ed. Homi Bhabha [New York: Routledge, 1990], 8–22); see also Renan, *Histoire générale*, esp. xv. For a discussion of Renan on race in terms that I have found most useful, see Jonathan Boyarin, "The Missing Keyword: Reading Olender's Renan," *Qui Parle* 7, no. 2 (spring/summer 1994): 43–56.

68. Renan, *Etudes d'histoire religieuse*, 88. Renan extends this line of argument regarding "the military inferiority of the Semites" all the way to the Algerian resistance of his days. To his mind "the most illustrious representative of the Semitic race today, Abd-el-Kader . . . is in no way a soldier" (89).

69. Renan, *Histoire générale*, 14.

70. Renan generously excludes some of his contemporary "Israëlites," who, although descending straight from ancient inhabitants of Palestine, are now simply "hommes modernes." Today, I assume, these would be the equivalent of "moderate Muslims"—the moderation of the modern in its relentless extermination of the "extreme" or "extremist."

71. G. W. F. Hegel, *Lectures on the History of Philosophy*, trans. E. S. Haldane and F. F. Simson (Lincoln: University of Nebraska Press, 1995), 3:1. On the importance of Hegel as setting the terms for a joined discussion of Jews and Arabs, Judaism and Islam, see my *The Jew, the Arab*, 120–133.

72. See Said, *Orientalism*, 286. The process whereby the Arab remains the only Semite is perhaps best illustrated by Philip K. Hitti, who in 1943 appears to see in that "fact" reason for both lament and pride, "monotonous uniformity" and "ethnic purity." "Of the two surviving representatives of the Semitic people," writes Hitti at a time when survival was already very much at issue, "the Arabs, in a larger measure than the Jews, have preserved the characteristic physical features and mental traits of the family. . . . The reasons which make the Arabian Arab, the nomad especially, the best representative of the Semitic family biologically, psychologically, socially and linguistically should be sought in his geographical isolation and in the monotonous uniformity of desert life. Ethnic purity is a reward of a most ungrateful and isolated environment" (Philip K. Hitti, *The Arabs: A Short History* [Chicago: Gateway, 1956], 6–7).

73. Susannah Heschel has described in eloquent terms the "liberation" Zionism attempts to effect, a liberation "from Judaism itself" (Heschel, "Revolt of the Colonized: Abraham Geiger's *Wissenschaft des Judentums* as a Challenge to Christian Hegemony in the Academy," *New German Critique* 77 (spring/summer 1999): 70; see also Heschel's *Abraham Geiger*.

74. See Raz-Krakotzkin, "Exile Within Sovereignty: Toward a Critique of the 'Negation of Exile' in Israeli Culture" [in Hebrew], *Theory and Criticism* 4–5 (1993): 23–56, 113–32; Massad, "The Post-Colonial Colony"; Boyarin, *Unheroic Conduct*; Oz Almog, *The Sabra: The Creation of the New Jew*, trans. Haim Watzman (Berkeley: University of California Press, 2000). In a related manner, for the past forty years or so, Jewish studies in America has been seeking, more or less successfully, to break away from its "Middle Eastern" or "Semitic" home departments, finding itself more comfortably housed in less racially marked (if silently so) departments of history or of religious studies.

75. "By an almost inescapable logic, I have found myself writing the history of a strange, secret sharer of Western anti-Semitism. That anti-Semitism and, as I have discussed it in its Islamic branch, Orientalism resemble each other very closely is a historical, cultural, and political truth that needs only to be mentioned to an Arab Palestinian for its irony to be perfectly understood" (Said,

Orientalism, 28). In case his nonironic readers fail to understand, Said repeats this later (and still, it did not help): "What has not been sufficiently stressed in histories of modern anti-Semitism has been the legitimation of [the] atavistic designations [deployed] by Orientalism, and more importantly for my purposes here, the way this academic and intellectual legitimation has persisted right through the modern age in discussions of Islam, the Arabs, or the Near Orient" (262).

76. Edward Said, once again, initiated what should have become an entire field of study when he wrote that "the transference of a popular anti-Semitic animus from a Jewish to an Arab target was made smoothly, since the figure was essentially the same" (Said, *Orientalism*, 286, 293). For a parallel argument that seeks to link, along different lines from those explored here, racism and anti-Semitism as coconstitutive of Europe, on the "verso" side of its concepts and, perhaps, nonconcepts, see Alain David, *Racisme et antisémitisme*. David also finds his inspiration in Derrida's work and underscores the importance of a vanishing, making the "troubling *constat* of an erasure of racism and anti-Semitism from the order of concepts" (50).

77. Ania Loomba, "'Delicious Traffick': Racial and Religious Difference on Early Modern Stages," in *Shakespeare and Race*, ed. Catherine M. S. Alexander and Stanley Wells (Cambridge, UK: Cambridge University Press, 2000), 206.

78. Julia Reinhard Lupton, quoted in ibid.

79. Ania Loomba, *Shakespeare, Race, and Colonialism* (Oxford: Oxford University Press, 2002), 45.

80. The citations are from Michael Lok's travel account, quoted in Loomba, *Shakespeare, Race, and Colonialism*, 47.

81. Jacques Derrida, "Racism's Last Word," in *"Race," Writing, and Difference*, ed. Henry Louis Gates Jr. (Chicago: University of Chicago Press, 1986), 330–331.

CHAPTER 2

1. Aamir Mufti, "Critical Secularism: A Reintroduction for Perilous Times," *boundary 2* 31, no. 2 (summer 2004): 3.

2. Edward W. Said, *The World, the Text, and the Critic* (Cambridge, MA: Harvard University Press, 1983), 29.

3. Bruce Robbins, "Secularism, Elitism, Progress, and Other Transgressions: On Edward Said's 'Voyage In,'" *Social Text* 40 (fall 1994): 26; and see Aamir R. Mufti, "Auerbach in Istanbul: Edward Said, Secular Criticism, and the Question of Minority Culture," *Critical Inquiry* 25 (autumn 1998): 95–125.

4. Nicholas B. Dirks, *Castes of Mind: Colonialism and the Making of Modern India* (Princeton, NJ: Princeton University Press, 2001).

5. Gauri Viswanathan, *Outside the Fold: Conversion, Modernity, and Belief* (Princeton, NJ: Princeton University Press, 1998), 45.

6. Mufti, "Critical Secularism," 3.

7. William D. Hart, *Edward Said and the Religious Effects of Culture* (Cambridge, UK: Cambridge University Press, 2000), 86.

8. Nadia Abu El-Haj, "Edward Said and the Political Present," *American Ethnologist* 32, no. 4 (Nov. 2005): 541.

9. Jonathan Z. Smith, "Religion, Religions, Religious," in *Critical Terms for Religious Studies*, ed. Mark C. Taylor (Chicago: University of Chicago Press, 1998), 281; for a proposal to substitute *religion* with *culture* see Richard King, *Orientalism and Religion: Postcolonial Theory, India, and "The Mystic East"* (London: Routledge, 1999); and Timothy Fitzgerald, *The Ideology of Religious Studies* (New York: Oxford University Press, 2000).

10. Edward W. Said, *Orientalism* (New York: Vintage, 1979), 23; see also Abu El-Haj, "Edward Said," 547–549.

11. Said, *The World*, 15.

12. Ibid.

13. Robbins, "Secularism," 27.

14. Talal Asad, *Formations of the Secular: Christianity, Islam, Modernity* (Stanford, CA: Stanford University Press, 2003), 25–26.

15. Said, *The World*, 14.

16. Said, *Culture and Imperialism* (New York: Vintage, 1993); Pierre Clastres, *La société contre l'état. Recherches d'anthropologie politique* (Paris: Minuit, 1974).

17. Jacques Derrida, "Faith and Knowledge: The Two Sources of 'Religion' at the Limits of Reason Alone," trans. Samuel Weber, in Jacques Derrida, *Acts of Religion*, ed. Gil Anidjar (New York: Routledge, 2002), 42–101; see also *Conversion to Modernities: The Globalization of Christianity*, ed. Peter van der Veer (New York: Routledge, 1996).

18. Serge Margel, *Superstition. L'anthropologie du religieux en terre de chrétienté* (Paris: Galilée, 2005).

19. Lynn White Jr., "The Legacy of the Middle Ages in the American Wild West," in *Speculum* 40, no. 2 (April 1965): 191; see also Mary Ann Perkins, *Christendom and European Identity: The Legacy of a Grand Narrative Since 1789* (Berlin: Walter de Gruyter, 2004).

20. Friedrich Nietzsche, *The Anti-Christ, Ecce Homo, Twilight of the Idols, and Other Writings*, ed. Aaron Ridley and Judith Norman (Cambridge, UK: Cambridge University Press, 2005).

21. See José Casanova, *Public Religions in the Modern World* (Chicago: University of Chicago Press, 1994). All of Casanova's "case studies" are, of course, Christian cases.

22. See Peter Harrison, *"Religion" and the Religions in the English Enlightenment* (Cambridge, UK: Cambridge University Press, 1990).

23. Talal Asad, *Genealogies of Religion: Discipline and Reasons of Power in Christianity and Islam* (Baltimore: Johns Hopkins University Press, 1993), 189–193.

24. See David F. Noble, *The Religion of Technology: The Divinity of Man and the Spirit of Invention* (New York: Penguin, 1999).

25. See Pierre Clastres, *La société contre l'état*, esp. chap. 11.

26. In addition to the writings mentioned in these notes, beginning with Talal Asad, I owe much of my understanding on this question to the work of Jean and John Comaroff, David Chidester, Peter van der Veer, and Tomoko Masuzawa, as well as, I will argue below, Edward Said.

27. Michel Foucault, *The History of Sexuality: An Introduction*, trans. Robert Hurley (New York: Vintage, 1990), 1:159.

28. Said, *Orientalism*, 82.

29. W. J. T. Mitchell, "Secular Divination: Edward Said's Humanism," in *Edward Said: Continuing the Conversation*, ed. Homi Bhabha and W. J. T. Mitchell (Chicago: University of Chicago Press, 2005), 99–108.

30. Said, *Orientalism*, 40–50, quoting R. W. Southern.

31. Ibid., 100.

32. Ibid., 95.

33. Ibid., 322.

34. Sven Lindqvist, *A History of Bombing*, trans. Linda Haverty Rugg (New York: New Press, 2001).

35. Said, *Orientalism*, 108, substituting "religion" for "the Orient."

36. Mufti, "Critical Secularism," 2; for a diametrically opposed view based on the same premises see Hart, *Edward Said*, 8.

37. See Richard Drinnon, *Facing West: The Metaphysics of Indian-Hating and Empire-Building* (Norman: University of Oklahoma Press, 1997).

38. Fitzgerald, *The Ideology of Religious Studies*, 6.

39. Said, *Orientalism*, 134. I correct Said's translation of "la science laïque" as "lay science" for obvious reasons of accuracy and emphasis.

40. Ibid., 115.

41. Ibid., 223.

42. Asad, *Genealogies*, 13.

43. Partha Chatterjee, *Nationalist Thought and the Colonial World*, in *The Partha Chatterjee Omnibus* (New Delhi: Oxford University Press, 1999), 17; and Margel, *Superstition*, 31.

44. See, e.g., Gauri Viswanathan, *Masks of Conquest: Literary Study and British Rule in India* (New Delhi: Oxford University Press, 1989).

45. Said, *Orientalism*, 2; further references will be made parenthetically in the text.

46. Tomoko Masuzawa, *The Invention of World Religions: Or, How European Universalism Was Preserved in the Language of Pluralism* (Chicago: University of Chicago Press, 2005), xi.

CHAPTER 3

1. Paul de Man, "Literary History and Literary Modernity," in *Blindness and Insight: Essays in the Rhetoric of Contemporary Criticism* (Minnesota: University of Minnesota Press, 1983), 145.

2. Ibid., 148. The paradigmatic example is no doubt women's literature, a debated corpus since it emerged on the American scholarly scene and elsewhere (see Elaine Showalter, *A Literature of Their Own: British Women Novelists from Brontë to Lessing* [Princeton, NJ: Princeton University Press, 1999]). In the last expanded edition Showalter gives her own account of the debates generated by her pioneering study. She points out that the book "helped create the new field of feminist literary history" (xv) and describes the site from which she writes as modern and novel. Her approach, she says, is "historical and cultural" (xx). Other fields have sought to establish historical specificity, even while grounding their argument—or their subject—in older traditions (see, e.g., the case of African American literature—a quintessentially modern "object"—as expounded by Henry Louis Gates Jr. in *The Signifying Monkey: A Theory of African-American Literary Criticism* [New York: Oxford University Press, 1988]; see also, for a very different appeal to modernity, one that reviews earlier such appeals, Brent Hayes Edwards, *The Practice of Diaspora: Literature, Translation, and the Rise of Black Internationalism* [Cambridge, MA: Harvard University Press, 2003]). For yet another perspective on European traditions see Gregory Jusdanis, *Belated Modernity and Aesthetic Culture: Inventing National Literature* (Minneapolis: University of Minnesota Press, 1991).

3. De Man, "Literary History," 152.

4. Jacques Derrida discusses the chances and risks of institutionalization around a name ("women") in "Women in the Beehive: A Seminar with Jacques Derrida," in *Men in Feminism*, ed. Alice Jardine and Paul Smith (New York: Routledge, 1989), 189–203. For an illuminating account of these issues and concerns in the specific case of Chinese literature, and of the function of the attribute "Chinese" and "Chineseness," see *Modern Chinese Literary and Cultural Studies in the Age of Theory: Reimagining a Field*, ed. Rey Chow [Durham, NC: Duke University Press, 2000]). In her introduction Chow demonstrates that the question of institutionalization is essential to any inquiry into "ethnic" or "national" and even "transnational" literature. Chow also engages Western sinol-

ogy as a field "ridden with the contradictions of a modernist, rationalist attempt to redeem the past" (13), an attempt that resonates with the processes I am here trying to describe in Hebrew and Jewish literary studies. Finally, Chow signals toward the "increasing noncoincidence between Chinese literary studies as such and what is actually taking place under its rubric" (16). This "noncoincidence," such as marked by the distinct terms *Hebrew* and *Jewish*, is precisely what I aim to explore in this chapter.

5. Réda Bensmaïa has powerfully argued for the originality, indeed, the inventiveness and creativity, of Francophone, specifically Maghrebi, literature. Interestingly enough, Bensmaïa's argument is less about the "modernity" of Francophone literature than about its distinctiveness, its production of works in French that "contribute to an understanding of the 'new world.'" Like Peggy Kamuf, who suggests that "history will have itself been inscribed within literature," Bensmaïa argues for an understanding of literature as experimental, as creative of "experimental nations," nations to "imagine or explore as if they were territories to rediscover and stake out, step by step, countries to invent and to draw while creating one's language" (Reda Bensmaïa, *Experimental Nations: Or, the Invention of the Maghreb* [Princeton, NJ: Princeton University Press, 2003], 8; see also Peggy Kamuf, *The Division of Literature or the University in Deconstruction* [Chicago: University of Chicago Press, 1997]).

6. De Man, "Literary History," 165.

7. In his Wellek Library Lectures Edward W. Said underscores the tragic links that, in addition to the obvious and overall pertinence of his analyses, make Paul de Man's work oddly relevant to our discussion of literary history and Hebrew and Jewish literatures. Said points out that "in the most offensive of his *Le soir* articles (March 4, 1941) de Man says that 'one thus sees that a solution of the Jewish problem which would aim at the creation of a Jewish colony isolated from Europe, would not entail deplorable consequences from the literary life of the West.' None of the commentators I have read," Said continues, "glosses one especially sinister resonance in the phrase 'the creation of a Jewish colony isolated from Europe.'" Indeed, no one else has noted this particular instance in which "in an anti-Semitic, brazenly collaborationist, and pro-Nazi paper an author seemed to be in fact not just recommending the Zionist project already underway . . . already entailing the onset of Palestinian dispossession, but to be doing so casually, almost backhandedly, as if the real subject was the health of Europe, not the disaster to be visited upon at least three generations of Palestinians" (Edward W. Said, *Musical Elaborations* [New York: Columbia University Press, 1991], 38). The tension (to say the least), between Zionist and Jew, between Hebrew and Jewish, could hardly be made more palpable.

8. Yitzhak Laor, "Schizolingua: Or, How Many Years Can Modern Hebrew

Remain Modern? On the Ideological Dictates of the Hebrew Language," in *Ideology and Jewish Identity in Israeli and American Literature*, ed. Emily Miller Budick (Albany: State University of New York Press, 2001), 214.

9. The phrase "narratives with no natives" is Laor's own translation of a Hebrew volume of essays on Israeli literature (Yitzhak Laor, *Anu kotvim otakh moledet: Masot 'al sifrut yisraelit* [Tel Aviv: Ha-kibbutz hame'uchad, 1995]). I am not suggesting, of course, that the conflicts that take place around literature in American universities and elsewhere are unimportant or marginal. In fact, the compelling argument made by Peggy Kamuf, whereby we must recognize that "literature, in effect, is instituted as a division and as such its institutional status is never fully assured," is at the very source of my endeavor here. Indeed, the word *division*, as Kamuf uses it, is meant to evoke the divisions and partitions, the wars and revolutions of which de Man writes and which literature "is" (Kamuf, *The Division of Literature*, 39).

10. This trend can be explained in a number of ways, not all of them scholarly, but be that as it may, it was initiated by my own institution, Columbia University, where "Israel and Jewish Studies" have long been placed under the same roof. Home to the first chair in Jewish History, the first position in Jewish studies in the Ivy League, Columbia has since become one of the major centers of Jewish studies in the country. It is also unique in having produced so early (1950) the institutional collapse of Jewish studies with Israel studies. (Note that it is "Israel studies" and not "Israeli studies" that names the endeavor. I am aware of no parallel use of a substantive rather than an adjective in such contexts—there is no such thing as "France studies," "Germany studies," or "Asia studies." With this gesture the State, rather than its different cultural sites, is augmented and appears to have imposed itself at once as object and title of the scholarly enterprise, this at a time when other national literatures and cultures have come under increasing, critical attention, and calls are issued for them to justify their continued existence.)

11. See Hannan Hever, "A Map of Sand: From Hebrew Literature to Israeli Literature" [in Hebrew], in *Teoria ve-bikoret* 20 (spring 2002): 165–190.

12. Arnold Band, "Jewish Literature in the University," in *Studies in Modern Jewish Literature* (Philadelphia: Jewish Publication Society, 2003), 378–379. The history of the relation between Yiddish and Hebrew literature has made an enormous leap since Band wrote these lines in 1962. The works of Dan Miron and Benjamin Harshav, of Ruth Wisse, Naomi Seidman, Chana Kronfeld, and many others, have contributed much to a deeper and richer understanding of the two distinct bodies of texts and languages. They have done so without yet altering the more general question of "Jewish literatures" in their relation to the now overwhelming hegemony of Hebrew, and particularly Modern Hebrew, literature.

13. Dan Miron, "Modern Hebrew Literature: Zionist Perspectives and Israeli Realities," in *What Is Jewish Literature?* ed. Hana Wirth-Nesher (Philadelphia: Jewish Publication Society, 1994), 95.

14. De Man, "Literary History," 161.

15. Gershon Shaked, *Gal hadash ba-siporet ha-'ivrit* (Tel-Aviv: Sifriyat Po'alim, 1970), 7. Robert Alter proceeds along the same lines when he titles a series of lectures *The Invention of Hebrew Prose*. The precision is made only in the subtitle, which does affirm the modern (Robert Alter, *The Invention of Hebrew Prose: Modern Fiction and the Language of Realism* [Seattle: University of Washington Press, 1988]).

16. Shaked, *Ha-siporet ha-'ivrit, 1880–1970* (Jerusalem: Keter, 1977), 13.

17. Alan Mintz, *Translating Israel: Contemporary Hebrew Literature and Its Reception in America* (Syracuse, NY: Syracuse University Press, 2001), 55.

18. Simon Halkin, *Modern Hebrew Literature from Enlightenment to the Birth of the State of Israel: Trends and Values* (New York: Schocken, 1970).

19. On "National Time" see Joseph Massad, *Colonial Effects: The Making of National Identity in Jordan* (New York: Columbia University Press, 2001), esp. 25–33; on the Form of the nation, and the nation as Form, see Stathis Gourgouris, *Dream Nation: Enlightenment, Colonization, and the Institution of Modern Greece* (Stanford, CA: Stanford University Press, 1996).

20. "Zionism equated cultural freedom with political independence, and therefore prescribed linguistic 'normalcy' as the only base for a full-fledged artistic literature. The great Hebrew masters of the first quarter of the twentieth century, some of whom were ardent Zionists, demonstrated that such 'normalcy' was not an artistic *sine qua non*" (Miron, "Modern Hebrew Literature," 101).

21. See Homi Bhabha, *The Location of Culture* (New York: Routledge, 1994), 145.

22. As will become clear, this institutional, pedagogical situation may be construed as distinct and even as opposed to the writing of the history of Modern Hebrew literature insofar as the novelty of the latter seems to have granted it autonomy. But one could also argue that no history of Modern Hebrew literature, as radical as it may be in distinguishing between ancient and modern (compare for example Halkin—"Modern Hebrew literature is the product of the last two hundred years of Jewish life" [Halkin, *Modern Hebrew Literature*, 15]—to Fischel Lachover, who immediately traces a longer history of softer transitions [Y. Fischel Lachover, *Toledot ha-sifrut ha-'ivrit ha-hadashah* [Tel-Aviv: Devir, 1955], 1]), ever ignores the past that preceded its development or appearance on the historical scene, favoring either biblical, rabbinical, medieval, renaissance, or all of the above (indeed, and to continue with him, Halkin argued in fact for the continuous engagement of Hebrew literature with its Jewish past). Yet that

relative autonomy leaves no doubt as to the definition of the field as "modern" and new, thus standing in tension with the *longue durée*, if one could call it that, of the pedagogical approach.

23. Consider the following difference with the field of Jewish history: the most important and well-known Jewish historians of modern times have been primarily scholars of medieval history (the "Jewish Middle Ages" extending, according to some, all the way to 1492 and even to the Enlightenment) such as Yitzhak Baer, Benzion Dinur, HaimHillel Ben-Sasson, Yosef Hayim Yerushalmi, and most important, Gershom Scholem. Recent scholarship has shown, moreover, that these historians were more than academic scholars. They shaped the national discourse to an extraordinary extent. In comparison, literary medievalists such as David Yelin, Hayim Schirmann, Ezra Fleischer, Dan Pagis, and Yosef Dan are important scholars, period. Pagis was also a significant public figure, but that is related to his extraordinary work as a poet. On these issues and more see the continuing and important work of Amnon Raz-Krakotzkin.

24. G. W. F. Hegel, *Phenomenology of Spirit*, trans. A. V. Miller (Oxford: Oxford University Press, 1977).

25. For a discussion of the relation between Hebrew modernism and the "new Jew" see Ariel Hirschfeld, "Locus and Language," in *Cultures of the Jews: A New History*, ed. David Biale (New York: Schocken, 2002), 1011–1062.

26. Hence, in the year 2000 Ruth Wisse was (finally? still?) advocating for the recognition of a "Jewish canon"—"I *propose* that . . . a modern Jewish canon has come into existence" (Ruth Wisse, *The Modern Jewish Canon: A Journey Through Language and Culture* [New York: Free Press, 2000], 3; emphasis added)—and that the study of this canon, which, surprisingly, *includes* Modern Hebrew and Israeli literature as one of its subdivisions, would attend to "the phenomenon of a multilingual Jewish literature." Wisse leaves little hope, however, for the medievalist literary critic as she too insists on the modern, and on building "the *modern* Jewish canon," as the title of her book has it. One should note that in mentioning the linguistic richness of what she calls "Jewish languages," Wisse includes "Yiddish and Ladino and Judaeo-Persian" (6). Not Judeo-Arabic and much less Arabic. Wisse knows of Albert Memmi but not of Yaqub Sanuʿ or of Samir Naqqash. Nor does she recall Edmond Jabès or Edmond Amran El Maleh, and much less, but this goes without saying, Yehuda ha-Levi. Not to speak, finally, of Anton Shammas. Inclusiveness at its limits.

27. Each of these departments has a different history, of course. Suffice it to say that, for overdetermined reasons, the Jewish Theological Seminary's particular commitment to Jewish history and to Jewish life has led it to develop its own historical approach to Jewish history and to Jewish literature. The JTS has, moreover, carefully negotiated its relationship to Zionism and to Israel, refrain-

ing from opening an Israeli branch for many years. As for Bar-Ilan University, it is a unique institution, the only Jewish Orthodox university. Its department of Jewish literatures ("Literatures of the Jewish People") was founded by Baruch Kurzweil, one of the staunchest proponents of the "crisis as rupture" thesis (a crisis profusely lamented as signifying, or at least announcing, the end of Judaism) and a very important if controversial literary critic.

28. The history of Jewish Studies in the United States would no doubt be relevant to explore here, and I have alluded to it earlier. The first two appointments made in Jewish Studies were Harry Austryn Wolfson (at Harvard, as Professor of "Hebrew [*sic*] Literature and Philosophy," in 1925) and Salo Wittmayer Baron (at Columbia, the first Professor of "Jewish History," in 1930). Interestingly enough, the phrase "Hebrew literature" in Wolfson's position had little to do with Hebrew or with literature: Wolfson, it may be recalled, is the great scholar of Philo, of the Arabic Kalam, and of Spinoza.

29. Miron, "Modern Hebrew Literature," 95.

30. Highly pertinent to my argument is Feldman's opening sentence: "Although the modern Hebrew woman writer has yet to find her literary historian, her first century may be demarcated as spanning the years 1897–1997" (Yael S. Feldman, *No Room of Their Own: Gender and Nation in Israeli Women's Fiction* [New York: Columbia University Press, 1999], 1).

31. It is remarkable that the rich collection of essays edited by Hana Wirth-Nesher does not constitute a call for institutionalization. Jewish literature is the object of a debate to which a number of individuals contribute; "some are affiliated with Israeli universities, others with universities in Europe or the United States" (H. Wirth-Nesher, "Defining the Undefinable: What Is Jewish Literature?" in *What Is Jewish Literature?* 11). I already mentioned Ruth Wisse's recent call for the acknowledgment that there *is* a modern Jewish canon. There are no appeals to create positions, to initiate programs of research, or even to hold seminars or conferences on the topic. Such is not the case with "Israel studies" or with the teaching of Hebrew or of Jewish history. Positions are requested and created; funds are raised and conferences organized. The National Yiddish Book Center has recently taken upon itself to "identify" the one hundred "greatest works of Modern Jewish literature." Appealing to a number of scholars (none of whom, incidentally, hold positions officially identified, as it were, as Jewish literature, although a number of them do hold positions in *Yiddish* literature), that organization has therefore produced a list intended for the general public. Clearly, a kind of institutionalization is at work, yet it is not one that takes place in the university, nor is it one that appears to seek a future beyond itself. Once the list was produced, the project appeared to be completed.

32. As I have already suggested, the medieval Arab Jewish philosopher poet

Yehuda ha-Levi functions as an ideal cipher for the impossibility of such borders, articulating the movement from non-Jew to Jew (the famous conversion of the king of the Khazars), from Arabic to Hebrew, from philosophical prose to poetry, and more—though not necessarily in this order. Yehuda ha-Levi is a figure of "Arab Jewish Letters," which I have tried to describe in my *Our Place in al-Andalus: Kabbalah, Philosophy, Literature in Arab Jewish Letters* (Stanford, CA: Stanford University Press, 2002).

33. De Man, "Literary History," 153.

34. Writing from a different perspective, Yitzhak Laor, whose highly original and singularly courageous work, as a poet, critic, and political commentator, is perhaps unmatched in Israel, endorses a similar, empirical argument against literary Hebrew and Hebrew literature as a whole. Except for rare examples, Laor explains, "the writer who lives and writes Hebrew in Israel . . . belongs to the elite and identifies with the language that erases the others." The Hebrew writer, in other words, ignores the different dialects and languages that are operating in one way or another in Israeli culture, in Hebrew as it is spoken and practiced by the population of the State, be it Ashkenazi, Mizrahi, or Palestinian. Laor pointedly asks whether that writer, or Hebrew literature as a whole (including departments of Hebrew literature), "gains anything by turning a deaf ear or a dull tongue to the languages that have been made to disappear" (Laor, "Schizolingua," 231). Clearly, Laor's argument is essential to retain and ponder.

35. Avital Ronell has elaborated a compelling argument tracing the links between literature and war in her *Stupidity* (Urbana: University of Illinois Press, 2002), esp. 3–29.

36. In the article I mentioned earlier, Arnold Band had already made the important suggestion that "written in different languages, in different cultural milieux and in different centuries, Jewish literature by itself is a perfect paradigm of comparative literature, by which we mean a concept of literature which evolves from the study of several literatures, each in itself and in comparison with the others" (Band, "Jewish Literature in the University," 372). Leaving aside the troubling question of paradigm as well as the matter of defining boundaries between self and other, it is important to note that Band proceeds to qualify his own suggestion by inscribing clear hierarchies. "Even more than Jewish literature throughout the ages," he writes, "modern Hebrew literature included all the major components of a body of literature which lends itself to comparative treatment" (380). Modern Hebrew literature would thus be (or had been—Band curiously writes of it in the past tense), *more* paradigmatic, more inclusive of the components necessary for a comparative treatment. It is unclear why this might be the case, nor is it at all clear why such a claim would be made in a lecture entitled "Jewish Literature in the University."

37. With this disappearance, and keeping in mind the oft-made comparisons between Hebrew and Sanskrit, I want partly to signal toward Sheldon Pollock's fruitful argument about "the death of Sanskrit." In Pollock's pertinent description the death of Sanskrit was accompanied by a larger phenomenon, namely, that "the mental and social spheres of Sanskrit literary production grew ever more constricted, and the personal and this-worldly, and eventually even the presentist-political, evaporated, until only the dry-sediment of religious hymnology remained" (Sheldon Pollock, "The Death of Sanskrit," *Comparative Studies in History and Society* 43, no. 2 [2001]: 417).

38. Friedrich Nietzsche, "On the Uses and Abuses of History," quoted in de Man, "Literary History," 149.

CHAPTER 4

1. My title is meant as an homage to the nineteenth-century attempt at describing the phenomenon that will be of interest to us here, namely, the relation between Hebrew and Arab narrative. I am referring to Moritz Steinschneider's ever-more-distant *Die Arabische Literatur der Juden: Ein Beitrag zur Literaturgeschichte der Araber* (Frankfurt am Main: J. Kauffmann, 1902). Steinschneider's detailed catalog of what he calls *at once* "the Arabic literature of the Jews" and "a literary history of the Arabs" is perhaps difficult to imagine today. Hence the importance of returning to works such as his and others, works of a very concrete, yet fabulous, imagination. The first part of my title cites Abraham Shalom Yahuda, *'Ever va-'Arav* (New York: Ogen, 1946), another unique instance of the scholarly imagination at work.

2. Roland Barthes, "Introduction à l'analyse structurale des récits," in Roland Barthes et al., *Poétique du récit* (Paris: Seuil, 1977), 7–8; trans. Stephen Heath in Barthes, *Image, Music, Text* (New York: Hill and Wang, 1977), 79.

3. Avital Ronell reads Kafka reading Abraham, Sarah, and Isaac in *Stupidity* (Urbana: University of Illinois Press, 2002), 287–294.

4. Vladimir Propp, *Morphology of the Folktale*, trans. Laurence Scott, 2nd ed., rev. and ed. Louis A. Wagner (Austin: University of Texas Press, 1968), 39.

5. Fethi Benslama, *La psychanalyse à l'épreuve de l'Islam* (Paris: Aubier, 2002), 124.

6. Gen. 2:24. Jacques Derrida offers the secret of the relation between God and Abraham, and between Abraham and his son, as the "secret of literature," the narrative of its untold origins, "as if the essence of literature, *stricto sensu*, in the sense that this word guards still in the West, was not essentially Greek but Abrahamic" (Jacques Derrida, *Donner la mort* [Paris: Galilée, 1999], 177). In another register Erich Auerbach had engaged in a similar reinscription of the Jew

Greek (Erich Auerbach, *Mimesis: The Representation of Reality in Western Literature*, trans. Willard R. Trask [Princeton, NJ: Princeton University Press, 1953]).

7. Edward Said, *The World, the Text, and the Critic* (Cambridge, MA: Harvard University Press, 1983), 16–17.

8. Ibid., 19; Said is quoting Ian Watt.

9. On fathers and forefathers, fathers and grandfathers, see Jacques Derrida, *The Postcard: From Socrates to Freud and Beyond*, trans. Alan Bass (Chicago: University of Chicago Press, 1987).

10. Qur'an 26:69–77, "The Poets," trans. Muhammad Asad.

11. Abraham S. Halkin, "Judeo-Arabic Literature," in *The Jews: Their Religion and Culture*, ed. Louis Finkelstein (New York: Schocken, 1971), 121.

12. The literature addressing the fact of translation, the enormous body of translated texts, circulating among Arabic, Hebrew, and Latin, is as extensive as our topic, which it replicates, in one way or the other. Less is known about polemics between Islam and Judaism, although the case of Yehuda ha-Levi—to whom we will return—has gained some exposure. For a survey and bibliography on the issue see Moshe Perlmann, "The Medieval Polemics Between Islam and Judaism," in *Religion in a Religious Age*, ed. S. D. Goitein (Cambridge, MA: Association for Jewish Studies, 1974), 103–138. More recently see Theodore Pulcini, *Exegesis as Polemical Discourse: Ibn Hazm on Jewish and Christian Scripture* (Atlanta: Scholars Press, 1998).

13. Lucette Valensi, "Multicultural Visions: The Cultural Tapestry of the Jews of North Africa," in *Cultures of the Jews*, ed. David Biale (New York: Schocken, 2002), 895. For more on this area see Yosef Tobi, "The Flowering of Judeo-Arabic Literature in North Africa, 1850–1950," in *Sephardi and Middle Eastern Jewries*, ed. Harvey E. Goldberg (Bloomington: Indiana University Press, 1996), 213–225; see also the work of Haim Zafrani, Efraim Hazan, Joseph Chetrit, Guy Dugas, Ammiel Alcalay, and others.

14. For a broad survey of these issues see Ammiel Alcalay, *After Jews and Arabs: Remaking Levantine Culture* (Minneapolis: University of Minnesota Press, 1993). On Arab Jews in modern times see Ella Shohat, "The Invention of the Mizrahim," *Journal of Palestine Studies* 29, no. 1 (autumn 1999): 5–20; on Sama'wal see Adnan A. Husain, "Conversion to History: Negating Exile and Messianism in al-Samaw'al al-Maghribi's Polemic Against Judaism," *Medieval Encounters: Jewish, Christian, and Muslim Culture in Confluence and Dialogue* 8, no. 1 (2002): 3–34; on Sannu' see Irene L. Gendzier, *The Practical Visions of Ya'qub Sanu'* (Cambridge, MA: Harvard University Press, 1966); on Palestinian writers and their relation to Hebrew see Hannan Hever, "Hebrew in an Israeli Arab Hand: Six Miniatures on Anton Shammas's *Arabesques*," in *The Nature and Context of Minority Discourse*, ed. A. JanMohamed and D. Lloyd (Oxford:

Oxford University Press, 1990), 264–293; Ibrahim Taha, *The Smile of an Optimistic Lover: A Comparative Reading of the Hebrew and Palestinian Novel in Israel* [in Hebrew] (Tel Aviv: Hakibbutz hameuchad, 1999); Salma Khadra Jayyusi, "Introduction: Palestinian Literature in Modern Times," in *Anthology of Modern Palestinian Literature*, ed. S. K. Jayyusi (New York: Columbia University Press, 1992), 1–80; Reuven Snir, "'Hebrew as the Language of Grace': Arab-Palestinian Writers in Hebrew," *Prooftexts* 15 (1995): 163–183; and Rachel Feldhay Brenner, "'Hidden Transcripts' Made Public: Israeli Arab Fiction and Its Reception," *Critical Inquiry* 26 (autumn 1999): 85–108; on the image of Arabs in Hebrew literature see Risa Domb, *The Arab in Hebrew Prose, 1911–1948* (London: Valentine Mitchell, 1982); and Gila Ramras-Rauch, *The Arab in Israeli Literature* (Bloomington: Indiana University Press, 1989); on Iraqi Israeli writers and their Arab Jewishness see Nancy E. Berg, *Exile from Exile: Israeli Writers from Iraq* (Albany: State University of New York Press, 1996); for a partial bibliography see Shmuel Moreh, *Arabic Works by Jewish Writers, 1863–1973* (Jerusalem: Ben-Zvi Institute, 1973); the catalog of Andalus, the Israeli publishing house dedicated to translating Arabic literature into Hebrew, constitutes a major testimony to the issues described in this chapter (see www.andalus.co.il/).

15. Within the parameters of this chapter it is no doubt most relevant to mention the work of Rina Drory, particularly her *The Emergence of Jewish-Arabic Literary Contacts at the Beginning of the Tenth Century* [in Hebrew] (Tel Aviv: Hakibbutz hameuchad, 1988) and *Models and Contacts: Arabic Literature and Its Impact on Medieval Jewish Culture* (Leiden: Brill, 2000). Consider the movement away from what Steinschneider called "the Arab literature of the Jews," with the distance between the two "identities" made more and more insistent (from literature to culture, and from culture to religion, from Arab-Jewish symbiosis to Jewish-Muslim symbiosis and culminating, ultimately, with Bernard Lewis's *The Jews of Islam*).

16. Reuven Firestone, *Journeys in Holy Land: The Evolution of the Abraham-Ishmael Legends in Islamic Exegesis* (Albany: State University of New York Press, 1990), 4–5. I am unable here to enter further into the dispute alluded to in the previous note, a dispute predicated on the claim to distinguish between language, race, ethnicity, culture, religion, and so forth. Each of these terms is highly contentious and is being refashioned on a constant basis, and more and more as I write. Suffice it to say that distinctions and differences matter, as should become clear in the course of the exposition that follows, but they do not matter in the same way at all times, nor is the way in which categories and distinctions are made (and the purposes for which they are made or insisted on) historically stable. My contribution here is but one moment in a longer reflection on the Jew, the Arab, most of which is, however, only marginally relevant here.

17. Reuven Firestone, "Jewish Culture in the Formative Period of Islam," in *Cultures of the Jews*, ed. David Biale (New York: Schocken, 2002), 280.

18. Aziz al-Azmeh, *Muslim Kingship: Power and the Sacred in Muslim, Christian, and Pagan Polities* (London: I. B. Tauris, 1997), xv.

19. On the relation between narrative, history, and power in a context highly relevant to us here see Aziz al-Azmeh, "Histoire et narration dans l'historiographie arabe," in *Annales ESC* 2 (mars–avril 1986): 411–431.

20. The editors of this anthology, which covers material from rabbinic times all the way to the nineteenth century, refer to the "Hebrew *maqama*" as being "modeled upon an Arabic genre." See *Rabbinic Fantasies: Imaginative Narratives from Classical Hebrew Literature*, ed. David Stern and Mark J. Mirsky (Philadelphia: Jewish Publication Society, 1990), 25; see also 253–256. For a significantly different perspective on Arab Jewish literature see Drory, *The Emergence*; and Drory, *Models and Contacts*.

21. S. D. Goitein, *Jews and Arabs: Their Contacts Through the Ages* (New York: Schocken, 1955), 197.

22. William M. Brinner, introduction to Nissim ben Jacob Ibn Shahin, *An Elegant Composition Concerning Relief After Adversity*, trans. W. M. Brinner (New Haven, CT: Yale University Press, 1977), xvi–xvii. For a similar argument see Raymond Scheindlin, who suggests that the term *Judeo-Arabic* "is useful far beyond the domain of language, for the Arabic character of the Jewish culture we are describing is evident not only in the Jews' use of the Arabic language but also in every aspect of their culture during the heyday of premodern Islam—even in their practice of religion and in the ways in which they used Hebrew" (Raymond P. Scheindlin, "Merchants and Intellectuals, Rabbis and Poets: Judeo-Arabic Culture in the Golden Age of Islam," in *Cultures of the Jews*, ed. David Biale [New York: Schocken, 2002], 317). Scheindlin further explains that "the Arabic spoken by the Jews did not differ markedly from that spoken by Muslim[s] in this period" (329), whereas "for the purpose of writing, the Jews used several different registers of Arabic" (330).

23. Goitein, *Jews and Arabs*, 47.

24. M. J. Kister, quoted in Ronald L. Nettler, "Early Islam, Modern Islam, and Judaism: The *Isra'iliyyat* in Modern Islamic Thought," in *Muslim-Jewish Encounters: Intellectual Traditions and Modern Politics*, ed. R. L. Nettler and S. Taji-Farouki (Amsterdam: Harwood Academic Publishers, 1998), 4. The verse from the Qur'an is, "O you who have attained to faith! Surrender yourselves wholly unto God, and follow not Satan's footsteps, for, verily, he is your open foe" (trans. Muhammad Asad).

25. Firestone, *Journeys*, 13.

26. Ibid., 14.

27. M. R. Rida, quoted in Nettler, "Early Islam," 6.

28. Nettler, "Early Islam," 9.

29. Although I will not specifically address the matter of narrative in philosophical writing, it should be pointed out that *allegory* (a contentious term, if not always contentious enough), and therefore narrative, traverses all the fields of writing on which I am touching; hence, in an elaborate discussion on the matter Frank Talmage describes allegory as "a characteristic feature of medieval Jewish literature" (see Frank Talmage, "Apples of Gold: The Inner Meaning of Sacred Texts in Medieval Judaism," in *Jewish Spirituality: From the Bible to the Middle Ages*, ed. Arthur Green [New York: Crossroad, 1989], 313–355); see also Isaak Heinemann, "Scientific Allegorization During the Jewish Middle Ages," in *Studies in Jewish Thought*, ed. A. Jospe (Detroit, MI: Wayne State University Press, 1981), 247–269.

30. Arthur M. Lesley, "A Survey of Medieval Hebrew Rhetoric," in *Approaches to Judaism in Medieval Times*, ed. David R. Blumenthal (Chico, CA: Scholars Press, 1984), 113. Lesley considers the subsequent impact of these changes when he asserts that "several kinds of Hebrew writing that originated in this period developed later, in Christian Europe, even after contact with Arabic ceased" (ibid.). If the story of Arab Jewish letters had many beginnings, it will only find its end with great difficulties, although such ends have been repeatedly announced.

31. Ibid., 111.

32. Ibid., 116.

33. Ibid.

34. Peggy Kamuf, *The Division of Literature or the University in Deconstruction* (Chicago: University of Chicago Press, 1997).

35. On Ibn 'Ezra see Raymond P. Scheindlin, "Rabbi Moshe Ibn Ezra on the Legitimacy of Poetry," in *Medievalia et Humanistica*, n.s., 7 (1976): 101–115; see also Joseph Dana's extended study addressing Arab precedents (Joseph Dana, *Poetics of Medieval Hebrew Literature According to Moshe Ibn Ezra* [in Hebrew] [Tel-Aviv: Dvir, 1982]); on Aristotle and Ibn 'Ezra see Yosef Tobi, "Aristotle's Poetics and Medieval Hebrew Poetry" [in Hebrew], *Dapim le-mehqar be-sifrut* 8 (1992): 107–122. On Maimonides' work on logic and rhetoric see Joel L. Kraemer, "Maimonides on the Philosophic Sciences in His Treatise on the Art of Logic," in *Perspectives on Maimonides*, ed. J. L. Kraemer (Oxford: Oxford University Press, 1991), 77–104.

36. It is important to consider that according to the famous Arab Jewish writer and translator Yehuda al-Harizi, Ibn Saqbel's work belongs to a long chain of poets, and the poet was himself learned in "the art of poetry [*melekhet ha-shir*]" (Yehuda al-Harizi, *Tahkemoni*, ed. I. Toporowsky [Tel-Aviv: Mahbarot le-

sifrut, 1952], 45). Literary criticism has a long history, and in this case it does not indicate the relevance of genres.

37. To my knowledge, the only compelling discussion of the literary proximity that links the two authors is Samuel M. Stern, "Rationalists and Kabbalists in Medieval Allegory," *Journal of Jewish Studies* 6, no. 2 (1955): 73–86. Engaging narrative and allegory, Stern's contribution is directly relevant to the issue of classical narratives.

38. Lesley, "Medieval Hebrew Rhetoric," 121. Before Lesley, Dan Pagis, the single most important literary critic of Hebrew medieval literature, had asserted that "the problem of genres in this field seems to have been touched upon only in incidental notes. . . . Not that the scholars ignored genres as such; on the contrary, they often mentioned individual pieces or larger collections as anecdotes, beast fables, beast epics, parables, novellas, novels, fabliaux, exampla, and above all maqamas. But they rarely bothered to examine the principle of such classifications, and variously attributed one work to different genres, sometimes even calling it in the same breath a maqama and a novel, or, say, a fable and an epic" (Dan Pagis, "Variety in Medieval Rhymed Narratives," in *Studies in Hebrew Narrative Art Throughout the Ages*, ed. J. Heinemann and S. Werses (Jerusalem: Magnes Press, 1977), 83. Since Pagis and Lesley wrote, the major exceptions to this state of affairs and implicit response to Lesley's call are Ross Brann, *The Compunctious Poet: Cultural Ambiguity and Hebrew Poetry in Muslim Spain* (Baltimore: Johns Hopkins University Press, 1991); and Rina Drory, *Models and Contacts: Arabic Literature and Its Impact on Medieval Jewish Culture* (Leiden: Brill, 2000). Note that Brann remains resolutely "secular" in his approach and in the material he engages.

39. Lesley, "Medieval Hebrew Rhetoric," 127.

40. David Stern, introduction to *Rabbinic Fantasies: Imaginative Narratives from Classical Hebrew Literature*, ed. David Stern and Mark J. Mirsky (Philadelphia: Jewish Publication Society, 1990), 13. On the issue of the Zohar's place in literary history and a more detailed elaboration on the questions I am here raising, see my *"Our Place in al-Andalus": Kabbalah, Philosophy, Literature in Arab Jewish Letters* (Stanford, CA: Stanford University Press, 2002), esp. 166–245.

41. Zohar 3:152a, translated and quoted by David Stern in Stern and Mirsky, *Rabbinic Fantasies*, 5.

42. Stern, introduction, 5. For a reading similar to Stern's, which recognizes the literary significance and impact of the Zohar in terms of the narrative imagination while reducing its own literary and narrative dimension, see J. Dan, *The Hebrew Story in the Middle Ages* [in Hebrew] (Jerusalem: Keter, 1974), 7–14.

43. Stern, introduction, 13.

44. Alcalay, *After Jews and Arabs*, 180.

45. al-Harizi, *Tahkemoni,* 11; English translation is from *The Tahkemoni,* trans. Victor E. Reichert (Jerusalem: Raphael Haim Cohen, 1965), 34–35. As Rina Drory underscores in her extended analysis of these passages, the author/narrator will then go on to reiterate this polemical view in a significantly different manner, confirming that "it is true that the Arabic language is the choicest of all tongues—the last and the first—[*ki leshon 'arab mivhar kol ha-leshonot, ha-aharonot veha-rishonot*], all others are different by contrast to it and their rules are different, and their words are despised and strange," to which he adds: "except for the Holy Tongue," namely, Hebrew (21/E47); and see Rina Drory, "Literary Contacts and Where to Find Them: On Arabic Literary Models in Medieval Jewish Literature," *Poetics Today* 14, no. 2 (summer 1993): 277–302.

46. al-Harizi, *Tahkemoni,* 9/E32.

47. Ibid., 12/14/E36–39.

48. Solomon Ibn Saqbel, "Ne'um Asher ben Yehuda," in *Hebrew Poetry in Spain and in Provence,* ed. H. J. Schirmann (Jerusalem: Bialik Institute, 1959), 1:565; English translation is from Scheindlin, *Rabbinic Fantasies,* 264.

49. Yehuda ha-Levi, *Kitab ar-radd wad-dalil fid-din adh-dhalil,* ed. David H. Baneth (Jerusalem: Magnes Press, 1977), 1:1; partial translation from the *Kuzari,* trans. Hartwig Hirschfeld (New York: Schocken, 1964), 35.

50. Diana Lobel, *Between Mysticism and Philosophy: Sufi Language of Religious Experience in Judah Ha-Levi's Kuzari* (Albany: State University of New York Press, 2000), 13.

51. Ibid., 1.

52. Ibid., 5.

53. Scheindlin, "Merchants and Intellectuals," 334; see also Drory, *Models and Contacts,* 158–177.

54. Scheindlin, "Merchants and Intellectuals," 344.

55. Ibid., 333.

56. *Kuzari,* 2:68, 79/E124–125.

57. I attend to this story in *"Our Place in al-Andalus,"* 177–189.

58. Moses Maimonides, *Guide of the Perplexed,* trans. Shlomo Pines (Chicago: University of Chicago Press, 1963), 2:29; I have commented at length on this passage in *"Our Place in al-Andalus,"* 10–44.

59. Shim'on Ballas, "Iya," trans. Susan Einbinder, in *Keys to the Garden: New Israeli Writing,* ed. Ammiel Alcalay (San Francisco: City Lights Books, 1996), 78.

60. Shim'on Ballas, "At Home in Exile: An Interview with Shim'on Ballas by Ammiel Alcalay," in *Keys to the Garden,* ed. Ammiel Alcalay (San Francisco: City Lights Books, 1996), 68.

61. Sami Shalom Chetrit, "Who Is a Jew and What Kind of a Jew?" in *Keys*

to the Garden, ed. Ammiel Alcalay (San Francisco: City Lights Books, 1996), 359–360.

62. S. D. Goitein, *Jews and Arabs*, 8. For a synthetic treatment of some of these transformations, addressing particularly the shift from ethnic categories to religious ones, see Steven M. Wasserstrom, *Between Muslim and Jew: The Problem of Symbiosis Under Early Islam* (Princeton, NJ: Princeton University Press, 1995). For a different perspective, focusing on Arab Jews in Israel, see Sami Shalom Chetrit, *The Mizrahi Struggle in Israel: Between Oppression and Liberation, Identification and Alternative, 1948–2003* (Tel Aviv: 'Am 'Oved, 2004); see also Ella Shohat, "The 'Postcolonial' in Translation: Reading Said in Hebrew," in *Journal of Palestine Studies* 33, no. 3 (spring 2004): 55–75, for a critique of Yehuda Shenhav's *The Arab Jews: A Postcolonial Reading of Nationalism, Religion, and Ethnicity* (Stanford, CA: Stanford University Press, 2006).

63. See, e.g., Harvey E. Goldberg, ed., *The Book of Mordechai: A Study of the Jews of Libya* (Philadelphia: Institute for the Study of Human Issues, 1980).

64. Shim'on Ballas, *The Other One* (Tel Aviv: Zmora-Bitan, 1991).

65. Abdelkebir Khatibi and Jacques Hassoun, *Le même livre* (Paris: Editions de l'Éclat, 1985).

66. In this context consider, for example, Fouzi El Asmar, *Through the Hebrew Looking-Glass: Arab Stereotypes in Children's Literature* (London: Zed Books, 1986).

67. Edmond Amran El Maleh, *Parcours immobile* (Paris: Maspero, 1980), 50.

68. Claude Kayat, *Mohammed Cohen* (Paris: Seuil, 1981). On Judeo-Maghrebian literature see Guy Dugas, *La littérature judéo-maghrébine d'expression française: Entre Djeha et Cagayous* (Paris: L'Harmattan, 1990). On Maghrebian literature, both French and Hebrew, see Ammiel Alcalay's groundbreaking study, *After Jews and Arabs*.

69. Guy Sitbon, *Gagou* (Paris: Grasset, 1980), 249.

70. Anton Shammas, *Arabesques*, trans. Vivian Eden (New York: Harper and Row, 1988), 92.

Cultural Memory | in the Present

Niklas Luhmann, *Theories of Distinction: Redescribing the Descriptions of Modernity*, ed. and introd. William Rasch

Johannes Fabian, *Anthropology with an Attitude: Critical Essays*

Michel Henry, *I Am the Truth: Toward a Philosophy of Christianity*

Gil Anidjar, *"Our Place in Al-Andalus": Kabbalah, Philosophy, Literature in Arab-Jewish Letters*

Hélène Cixous and Jacques Derrida, *Veils*

F. R. Ankersmit, *Historical Representation*

F. R. Ankersmit, *Political Representation*

Elissa Marder, *Dead Time: Temporal Disorders in the Wake of Modernity (Baudelaire and Flaubert)*

Reinhart Koselleck, *The Practice of Conceptual History: Timing History, Spacing Concepts*

Niklas Luhmann, *The Reality of the Mass Media*

Hubert Damisch, *A Childhood Memory by Piero della Francesca*

Hubert Damisch, *A Theory of /Cloud/: Toward a History of Painting*

Jean-Luc Nancy, *The Speculative Remark (One of Hegel's Bons Mots)*

Jean-François Lyotard, *Soundproof Room: Malraux's Anti-Aesthetics*

Jan Patočka, *Plato and Europe*

Hubert Damisch, *Skyline: The Narcissistic City*

Isabel Hoving, *In Praise of New Travelers: Reading Caribbean Migrant Women Writers*

Richard Rand, ed., *Futures: Of Derrida*

William Rasch, *Niklas Luhmann's Modernity: The Paradox of System Differentiation*

Jacques Derrida and Anne Dufourmantelle, *Of Hospitality*

Jean-François Lyotard, *The Confession of Augustine*

Kaja Silverman, *World Spectators*

Samuel Weber, *Institution and Interpretation: Expanded Edition*

Jeffrey S. Librett, *The Rhetoric of Cultural Dialogue: Jews and Germans in the Epoch of Emancipation*

Ulrich Baer, *Remnants of Song: Trauma and the Experience of Modernity in Charles Baudelaire and Paul Celan*

Samuel C. Wheeler III, *Deconstruction as Analytic Philosophy*

David S. Ferris, *Silent Urns: Romanticism, Hellenism, Modernity*

Rodolphe Gasché, *Of Minimal Things: Studies on the Notion of Relation*

Sarah Winter, *Freud and the Institution of Psychoanalytic Knowledge*

Samuel Weber, *The Legend of Freud: Expanded Edition*

Aris Fioretos, ed., *The Solid Letter: Readings of Friedrich Hölderlin*

J. Hillis Miller / Manuel Asensi, *Black Holes / J. Hillis Miller; or, Boustrophedonic Reading*

Miryam Sas, *Fault Lines: Cultural Memory and Japanese Surrealism*

Peter Schwenger, *Fantasm and Fiction: On Textual Envisioning*

Didier Maleuvre, *Museum Memories: History, Technology, Art*

Jacques Derrida, *Monolingualism of the Other; or, The Prosthesis of Origin*

Andrew Baruch Wachtel, *Making a Nation, Breaking a Nation: Literature and Cultural Politics in Yugoslavia*

Niklas Luhmann, *Love as Passion: The Codification of Intimacy*

Mieke Bal, ed., *The Practice of Cultural Analysis: Exposing Interdisciplinary Interpretation*

Jacques Derrida and Gianni Vattimo, eds., *Religion*